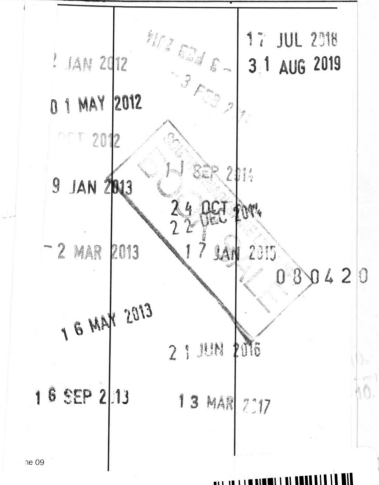

They belonged to Glasgow

THE CITY FROM THE BOTTOM UP

Rudolph Kenna & Ian Sutherland

www.nwp.co.uk

Neil Wilson Publishing Ltd
303a The Pentagon Centre
36 Washington Street
GLASGOW
G3 8AZ

Tel: 0141-221-1117
Fax: 0141-221-5363
E-mail: info@nwp.sol.co.uk
www.nwp.co.uk

A catalogue record for this book is available from the British Library.

ISBN 1-903238-32-3
Typeset in Palatino
Designed by Robbie Porteous
Printed by WS Bookwell

CONTENTS

Part II 1914-1945

Part III 1946-1978

Introduction

Although there have been many books on Glasgow, little attention has been paid to the ordinary men, women and children of the dear green place. In these pages we attempt to set the record straight.

In Part One we look at the city between 1751 and 1913, during which Glasgow experienced one of the most astonishing population explosions in history, fuelled – during the great age of expansion – by Highland migration and Irish immigration. Eighteenth-century Glasgow wasn't only a town of 'tobacco lords', haughty Virginia traders whose wives and daughters took elocution lessons and learned to play the guitar 'in good taste'. It was also a town of servants, beggars, whores, and thieves – the latter living precariously on their wits and risking draconian retribution in the form of floggings, banishment or capital punishment. Similarly Victorian Glasgow wasn't only a city of prosperous 'captains of industry', but also one where children slept rough and stole to obtain the bare necessities of existence – a place where whole families begged in the streets and many unfortunates sought oblivion in opiates or alcohol. The slums were honeycombed with brothels, shebeens, and 'wee pawns' where 'child-strippers' disposed of clothes stolen from infants and small children.

In Part Two we look at the city between 1914 and 1945 – tumultuous years when Glaswegians won medals, marched against unemployment and the Means Test, fought greedy landlords, befriended refugees from Nazi oppression and rescued fellow citizens from blitzed tenements. (They also ran brothels, wielded razors, distilled illicit spirits, cracked safes, and joined nudist clubs!)

In Part Three we turn our attention to the city between 1946 and 1978 – from post-war austerity to the eve of Thatcherism. It was a period when tens of thousands of Glaswegians were shunted from rat-infested inner-city slums to bleak peripheral housing schemes – famously described by comedian Billy Connolly as 'deserts wae windaes'. Thousands more went to Scotland's 'new towns' and ceased to 'belong to Glasgow'.

As the reader will discover, all sorts and conditions of people – brave, foolhardy, generous, eccentric, creative, crafty, vicious, intelligent, stupid, kind, decent, hypocritical, vile, mercenary, reactionary and revolutionary – belonged to the dear green place. The overwhelming majority never made it into the pages of orthodox history books. This publication is dedicated to their memory.

Rudolph Kenna and Ian Sutherland, 2001.

Part I
1751–1913

1751   Flea Circus

Impresario John Jarvis, Trongate, gave a series of evening entertainments in his flat. Attractions included 'an ivory coach drawn by a flea with great ease'. Helen Campbell, 'a Gypsy', was convicted of theft, whipped through the streets and banished from Glasgow 'by tuck of drum'. Thomas Harkless, an Irish 'strolling beggar', was charged with vagrancy. He was in possession of £19. Harkless was sent to the House of Correction and then deported to Ireland.

Forged halfpennies, 'coined at Birmingham of a very base metal', circulated in Glasgow. Fear was dud coins might turn up in Kirk collection plates. Smiths, joiners, shoemakers, tailors and other workers 'willing to enter into indentures for four years' were offered free passages on the good ship *Jenny*, from Irvine to South Carolina. A Glasgow merchant, riding home from Port Glasgow, was waylaid by a highwayman. Better mounted than his assailant, he galloped off – with a bullet hole in his hat.

1758   Ston'd Horse

James Graham, landlord of the White Horse Inn, Gallowgate, advertised a stallion called 'Young Othello' – described as 'a fine bay ston'd horse'. Mares were served at a guinea 'and a shilling to the keeper, ready money'. Alexander Paton, of the Leopard Inn, Glasgow Cross, charged a guinea for the services of his colt 'Farmour'. The horse – 'very fit for getting light-footed chaise-horses, cart-horses, or strong hunters' – was 'always at home'.

Janet Paterson was 'drummed out of Glasgow' for resetting stolen goods. 'She had a label on her breast and some stolen yarn about her neck.' Muggers, believed to be soldiers, attacked and robbed several people on the lonely country road between Glasgow and Anderston. James Knox, bookseller, Saltmarket, offered patent medicines, including 'a chymical preparation for pimples and other scorbutick outbreakings on the skin, ointment and powder for the hemorrhoids', and 'specific tincture for worms'.

1759   Pectoral Drops

Surgeon James Muir offered lectures on midwifery. 'No woman will be admitted to the lectures unless her character for sobriety and prudence is attested by some persons of reputation in the place she lives in'. 'Dr Bateman's Pectoral Drops' claimed to cure 'fluxes, spitting of blood, consumptions, agues, smallpox, measles, colds and coughs'. This elixir also purported to remedy 'the most racking torment of the gout' – and prevented miscarriages, cured rickets and 'brought away slime, gravel and sometimes stones of great bigness'. Dr Bateman also peddled 'The Original Daffy's Mixture', along with 'The Court or Ladies' Black Sticking Plaster'. He complained loudly that 'one Dicey' offered 'crude imitations'.

1760   Vicious Humours

Peter Patterson, a Glasgow shoemaker, offered £1 reward for the capture of his apprentice Malcolm Clark – 'well built, very black complexion, pitted with the smallpox'.

Messrs Pringle and Dick opened a dancing school in the British Coffee House Close, Glasgow Cross. Ladies were taught 12-2, gents 3-8. 'Mr Glaget', Morrison's Land, Briggait, offered 'instructions for performing on the citra or guitare in good taste'. £1 was offered for the capture of Patrick McMurphy – 'pock-pitted, down-looked' – who'd deserted from the army at Cumbernauld.

Miners demanded 'their wages raised in proportion as their masters raised the price of their coal'. Soldiers were brought in. Nine miners were imprisoned, but were quickly released. Mr Ritchie advertised for miners for his Craigton Colliery, Govan. 'At this work, a good collier may with ease earn above two shillings per day.' 'Dr Ratcliff's Purging Elixir' claimed to 'cleanse the body of all cross and vicious humours, contracted by heavy drinking'. It also 'cured' smallpox, King's Evil (scrofula), deafness, scurvy and dropsy.

Several prisoners escaped from Glasgow Tolbooth, including Alexander Thomson, son of a Gorbals innkeeper, doing time for assaulting an excise man. 'Mrs Home' opened a boarding school for young ladies, at her house in Bell's Wynd, High Street. Boarders paid £5 a quarter; day pupils paid ten bob. 'A gentlewoman lately come from London' established a 'French language school' for young ladies at her lodgings in Trongate.

There was launched *The Lady's Museum* – a new monthly magazine which contained 'a course of female education and a variety of other particulars for the information and amusement of the ladies'.

1764   Bloody Register

Glasgow was 'infected with a gang of villains, who, under cloud of night, attack people in the streets, carrying off hats, cloaks, or anything they can lay hold of'. A reward was offered for the capture of an 'Indian boy', who ran away from his master's house in Glasgow. He was about 14 years old, 'with a hole cut through each ear about half an inch long'. He was 'bare leg'd and bare footed, a farmer's hat on his head, a coarse very dark coat or frock, his vest of cloathe chocolate colour, and blew gray breeches'. Citizens were advised: 'The lad can scarce speak a word of English, and a little French tho' not good.'

City blacksmith Robert Craig, demonstrated his 'patent fire engine' which 'gave general satisfaction ... going easily over the highest houses'. *The Bloody Register*, a sensational new weekly magazine, featured 'the most remarkable tryals for murder, treason, rape, sodomy, highway robbery, pyracy, house-breaking, perjury, forgery, and other high crimes and misdemeanors'.

Messrs Kennedy and Martin, 'above the Cross', purveyed 'burial crapes and tartans for gouns and plaids'. William Gordon's Academy, Trongate, trained young men for 'mercantile and mechanical employments'. Subjects included 'all the branches of mathematical learning with the French and Italian languages'.
Health-conscious Glaswegians enjoyed the benefits of 'salt water and goat whey'. Holiday accommodation was available in 'the mansion house of Gourock ... As there is a turnpike road almost the whole way, the communication is equally good to Glasgow by land or water'.

1772   Prunelloes

'A frost ... more intense than has been known since the year 1740' gripped Glasgow. The Clyde was 'entirely frozen for many miles'. Magistrates offered five guineas reward for information leading to the arrest of the person or persons who'd smashed one of the lamps on Jamaica Bridge.

Ten guineas reward was put up for the capture of eight prisoners on the skite from the Tolbooth. William Barroch, a thief, was pilloried and afterwards 'drum'd out of town, and banished the city and liberties for life'. Dried coltsfoot leaves, boiled in spring water, was recommended as a cure for 'Hooping Cough'. 'Young military bloods' went into a tavern and 'wantonly kick'd up a dust, knock'd down the landlord, &c. and behav'd in a very riotous manner'. Alarmed by increasing burglaries, magistrates ordered constables to 'search for and apprehend all idle vagrants that shall be found lurking in and about the town'.

John Brechin, Glasgow Cross, flogged quarts of 'new drawn off Entire Butt Beer – sevenpence for beer and bottle'. Green tea was 12s per lb, Souchong 7s, and Bohea 3/4d. Ebenezer Erskine, Trongate, offered 'high colour'd bitter oranges', along with 'prunelloes and French plumbs'.

Also in Trongate, 'The Old Silk Shop' stocked 'fresh and fashionable goods ... sold very low for ready money'. 'Mr Peacock', waggoner, Gallowgate, sold 'the German wooden clocks ... of both the common and coockcow kind'. Leading citizens, worried by the number of shops selling gunpowder, petitioned for a powder magazine 'at a proper distance from the town'. Glaswegians were instructed to apprehend deserter James McLean – 'smooth and fair-faced, remarkably well made ... had on a full suit of blue cloaths, grey striped worsted stockings, and new channel pumps'. Factors – 'tacksmen' – were sought for 'Cowcaddens laigh park and Cowcaddens hill park'. Both were 'esteemed very fit for being converted into gardens'.

1774   Jesuit Drops

A New York gentleman wrote to a friend in Glasgow, describing the arrival of the brig *Nancy*, carrying evicted Highlanders from Sutherland to America. Emigrants had been 'treated with unparalleled barbarity'. Nearly 100 died during the voyage. Of 50 babies and infants, 49 were dead. Of seven women who gave birth on the ship, only one was alive. All new-born babies died. The captain 'narrowly escaped the vengeance of the law' by leaving port 'with his vessel in the night'.

In Glasgow's new theatre, at Grahamston (now Hope Street), Shakespeare's plays were presented, along with 'a new Scots pantomime called Harlequin Highlander, or a trip to Loch Lomond'. Mrs Arthur Stewart, Bell's Wynd, advertised 'all sorts of grave clothes, made up in the newest and neatest fashion as now used in Edinburgh'.

'Dr Walker's Patent Jesuit Drops', available from Forrester and Reid, Trongate, claimed to cure 'persons of both sexes afflicted with the venereal disease'.

1778   Unnatural Rebellion

Glasgow raised the Glasgow Royal Volunteers, 'to enable His Majesty to quell the present unnatural rebellion in America'. Civic dignitaries opened the subscription list with £1000. Professional and trade associations also subscribed large sums. Recruiting officers paraded with colours flying and drums beating, then adjourned to the Saracen's Head Inn, where they distributed free porter to the populace gathered round a huge bonfire in Gallowgate. Members of the 'Beggars Benison', a famous Glasgow club, offered volunteers a reward of five guineas on top of the standard military bounty. Recruits were given the Freedom of the City of Glasgow and were promised 'a certainty of being discharged at the end of three years, or at the end of the rebellion in America'. Some recruits spent their bounties – and then bunked off. John McCall, drover, 'black visaged, a little pitted with the smallpox, thick curled hair', deserted from the Volunteers – wearing 'a blue coat, red vest, blue breeches, and blue stockings, and a pair of strong black buckles in his shoes'.

At Jordanhill Colliery, a workman, 'in stepping out of the bucket, set his foot on a loose deal, and fell to the bottom of the pit, by which he was so miserably crushed, that he died, soon after, in great agony'.

William McNaught, a servant of Robert Napier, brewer at Grahamston, absconded with £20. At Camlachie Toll, McNaught changed a sixpence. The toll keeper noticed that he produced the coin 'from a large bag of silver'. The authorities thought McNaught was 'making for Edinburgh'.

1780   Surprising Giant

The council installed nine oil lamps in Trongate, between Tron Kirk and Stockwell Street. Glaswegians rioted over Parliamentary efforts to repeal discrimination against Catholics. A mob destroyed a shop in King Street and a pottery in Tureen Street, which belonged to 'Mr Bagnel, a Catholic'.

Mathew Johnston (25) deserted from a recruiting party in Glasgow. Irish-born, he was 'by trade a labourer, dark complexion, dark brown hair, grey eyes, smallpox pitted ... had on when he went away, a dark blue duffel slip coat ... a white cloth waistcoat, with carv'd yellow buttons, leather breeches, and a plain cocked hat wanting the button and loop'.

A grazier, en route for digs in Gorbals, 'was accosted by a girl of the town, who artfully picked his pocket upon the Old Bridge of a watch and some money'.

Magistrates told citizens to cease emptying 'nastiness' from windows. Parents were ordered to stop boys from playing shinty in the streets and on Glasgow Green. 'At the sign of the Civet Cat', Trongate, a hairdresser and perfumer sold 'French and English Pomatum', 'aromatic and plain teeth powders', 'Bear Grease', and 'a pomatum for destroying nits in the hair'.

'The Surprising Irish Giant' – 21 years old and eight feet tall – was on view in the Saracen's Head Inn 'for a few days only'.

1782   Peruke Makers

Archibald Paterson, candlemaker, Trongate, offered for sale 'good white soap' at sevenpence per pound, and 'good brown soap' at sixpence halfpenny per pound. Mr Fischer, who kept a porter cellar below the Star and Garter Tavern, Prince's Street, offered 'private families' draught porter at 3d per quart. He also had 'une grande chambre ecartee' for the use of clubs and societies. A hike in grain and hop prices obliged city brewers to increase the price of their porter and strong ale by 3d per gallon. As an additional economy measure, they discontinued their time-honoured practice of giving presents to their customers on New Year's Day.

A 'new caravan' ran between Glasgow and Edinburgh on Tuesdays, Thursdays and Saturdays. It left from Trongate; tickets 8s 6d. Angus McDonald, proprietor of the Universal Hardware and Jewellery Warehouse, head of Saltmarket, offered 'money for old gold, silver, and lace' and sold 'Fendon's Nervous Drops' and 'Maredant's Drops for the Scorbutic Humours'. William McFarlane, Boyd's Land, Trongate, advertised 'long hairs and wig-mounting for peruke makers'. Alexander Baillie, engraver, Trongate, gave drawing lessons as a sideline. Fee: half a guinea per month.

1783   Cock-Match

The city fathers threatened to 'make a public example' of the unknown person or persons who had 'wickedly, wantonly, and maliciously' smashed a large number of lamps in the town. Robert Calder, shoemaker, was banished 'by tuck of drum' for seven years for resetting stolen goods and enticing boys to steal. The brigantine Fly arrived in the Clyde from North Carolina with a cargo of tobacco. She was the first American vessel to arrive in port since the end of the War of Independence. A reward of five pounds was offered for the discovery of Margaret Bogg (21), who had 'run off' from the Glasgow bleachfield with a piece of linen ten yards long. Mr Brown, Argyle Street, offered for sale 'the best, cleanest, and purest violet-powder' for dressing hair.

A 'cock-match' featuring sixteen fighting cocks, took place in Joseph Payne's cockpit at Rutherglen Bridge-end. Hutcheson's Hospital sought positions as servants 'in town or country' for a number of young girls, aged between ten and fifteen. McNair's grocery establishment, Trongate, advertised 'a large parcel of lemons, sweet oranges, new figs, currants, &c., in wholesale and retail, at very moderate prices, for ready money'. For a fee of one guinea, citizens could have their fortunes told by 'the famous Don Pedro', Bridgegate ('he has travelled over most parts of the East, and has arrived at the greatest pitch of EASTERN LEARNING').

1785   Surprising Dwarf

For four months, Glasgow endured the 'Great Frost'. The Clyde was frozen until March 14. During the freeze-up, booths and dram shops were erected on the ice. Two 'extraordinary productions of nature' – 'The Surprising Dwarf ... the shortest person that has ever been exhibited to the public', and 'A Young Lady from Newfoundland, born without arms' – went on show at Mr Brown's Auction Room, Saltmarket.

Neil McLean forged guinea notes of the Glasgow Arms Bank and was sentenced to death. Counterfeit ha'pennies were also circulating – 'to the detriment of the lieges'. Two Calton weavers, John Pitcairn and William Hutton, were whipped through the town and permanently banished for stealing £8 3/10d and two pieces of ribbon. 'The lands of Upper Ibrox ... with a steading of substantial and convenient farm houses' were for sale. 'Mr & Mrs Bonnet' opened a dancing school in Stockwell Street – young ladies were taught in the mornings, young men during afternoons.

Italian balloonist Vincento Lunardi made an 'aerial voyage' from St Andrew's Churchyard. 'He ascended into the atmosphere with majestic grandeur, to the astonishment and admiration of an immense crowd of spectators.' Lunardi landed at Hawick – two and a half hours later. 'Mr Solomon', lodging in Trongate, promised to extract teeth 'with such facility, by the improved construction of instruments, as scarcely to give pain.' Smallpox killed 190 Glaswegians, 274 died of fever and 81 of 'teething'. Twenty-four women died of 'child-bed'.

1789   Hick-Cough

Citizens flocked to Fraser's Hall, King Street, to see 'Dr Katterfelto' demonstrate his 'wonderful new-invented solar microscope'. The good 'doctor' promised to 'show above 50,000 insects, as large as eels, in a drop of vinegar the size of a pin's head;

also 80,000 live insects in a drop of clear water, some as large as birds; likewise mites in cheese as large as rats, and 90,000 other uncommon and surprising objects'.

Among the patent medicines sold by J. Mennon, Trongate, were Godfrey's Cordial for fluxes and 'hick-cough', Hatton's Itch Water, Velnos Vegetable Syrup for apoplexies and palsies, and Cornwell's Vegetable Cordial for gout. In a duel, fought with pistols on Glasgow Green, both protagonists – a merchant and a lawyer – escaped without a scratch. The merchant's round 'grazed the curl of the lawyer's wig'. In another bloodless encounter between a weaver and a barber – fought in the Craig Park overlooking Glasgow Cathedral – the weaver's ball 'took away part of the barber's coat'. Kent & Son, King Street, proprietors of The Tea and Perfumery Warehouse, advertised 'London refined sugar, patent ready-made mustard, and essence of spruce for table-beer'. King Street also housed the Messrs D'Asti's Academy for 'drawing, fortification, fencing, and the French and German languages'.

The town council advertised for a jailor for the debtors' prison in the Tolbooth. The successful applicant was warned that he would be 'answerable for the safe custody of the prisoners, under the penalty of the debts and sums of money for which they are imprisoned'. The authorities sought the owners of two cows, found grazing 'on the lands of Sandyford, nigh the village of Anderston'. The Intendant of Police offered 'a handsome reward' for the discovery of thieves who broke into a city warehouse and escaped with 'a considerable parcel of chintz and purple shawls'. Alexander Kay, Trongate, offered for sale Madeira wine at 27s 6d per dozen bottles, 'ready money'.

A 'mercantile diligence' holding three passengers set out every day, Sundays excepted, from the Buck's Head Inn, Argyle Street, for Greenock. Fare 6s. Robert Arthur, distiller at St Enoch's Burn, sought 'a brewer in the aquavitae line ... None need apply but those of a good character, and can do their business well'. In Trongate, corner of Candleriggs, Henry Hemming opened the Glasgow Hotel, Coffee House and Tavern. The latest newspapers and magazines were available to subscribers, who paid £1per annum and 'one shilling the Waiter'.

1790   Woodside Farm

Coalowners in the vicinity of Glasgow 'having suffered much from the credit taken by many of their customers' – sold their coal 'for ready money only'. A vacancy arose for 'an experienced spinner of mule jeanie yarn'. Girls were offered apprenticeships 'to learn the art of tambour'. The Misses Brown, Trongate, offered to 'dress the dead in the most expeditious manner, in town or country'.

On July 7, the first direct mail coach from London arrived at the Saracen's Head Inn. Passengers were welcomed by flunkeys in crimson plush breeches and powdered wigs. 'The villa and lands of Kelvingrove ... perfectly retired, although within one mile of the city of Glasgow' were auctioned at the Tontine Tavern, Trongate. Also on offer was 'the farm of Woodside, surrounded on all hands by beautiful landscapes ... such a situation as is rarely to be met with'. The village of Partick advertised for 'a person who can teach English, Writing, Arithmetic, and Book-keeping. He will be accommodated with a school-house, dwelling-house, and large garden free, with some other emoluments'. Anderston weaver John McCowl was whipped through the streets and banished for life for stealing pieces of cloth from a bleachfield.

1793   Deranged Shapes

The British Lottery offered top prizes of £30,000, £20,000 and £10,000. Tickets and shares were sold in halves, quarters, eighths and sixteenths. The Tron Kirk was burnt down by the Hell-Fire Club – Hooray Henrys who indulged in drunken pranks. Agnes McCallum poisoned her five-month-old baby. She was hanged and her body sent for dissection. Famous corset-maker Monsieur Dutailles, 'arrived from Paris', lodging in Bell's Wynd, announced: 'Any lady with a deranged shape may be fitted with a very elegant stay, or corset, that will remedy all defects, and will be as easy to the wearer as any other stay whatever.'

McDonald's Patent Medicine Warehouse, Trongate, stocked 'Dr Hooper's Female Pills, Dr Steer's Purging Elixir, Dr Waite's Worm Nuts, and Cephalic Snuff'. Twelve French POWs en route via Glasgow from Greenock to Edinburgh were housed in Candleriggs guard-house. 'During their stay here their situation was not like prisoners, for they were amply provided with provisions.'

Mary Douglas stole sheets from a house in Bridgeton. She was whipped through the streets and banished for life. Glasgow Highland Society, based at the Black Bull Inn, Argyle Street, offered apprenticeships for 20 lads of Highland descent and provided clothing for the first three years of employment. The city sought a street-sweeper, offering a contract 'for one or more years.'

'The great bells of this city' were rung to celebrate the anniversary of Guy

Fawkes's downfall. 'A lady and her servant', walking to Charlotte Street via High Street, were attacked by 'Highland soldiers'. The assailants ran off in the direction of the Glasgow College.

1796   Young Boffka

A coach left the Black Bull Inn, Argyle Street, every weekday at 10am, travelling to Edinburgh via Airdrie and Bathgate. 'Inside tickets 10s and outsides 6s each'. Among the patent medicines offered for sale by John Buchanan at the Sun Fire Office, Glassford Street, was a nostrum for venereal disease – 'the most effectual remedy for that dreadful distemper ever found out, and never fails to cure the most desperate case in thirty-six hours, by only twice using'.

Mr Alex, 'dentist and corn operator' took lodgings in Trongate and advertised: 'Artificial teeth set to the greatest nicety; and hollow teeth filled up with gold, silver, or lead'. John Swanston & Co., Trongate, stocked a wide range of delicacies, including Spanish figs, China oranges, pickled walnuts, mushroom ketchup, Spanish olives, Muscatel raisins, 'maccarony', and 'vermicelly'. Archibald Campbell & Co., St Andrew's Street, took delivery of 140 hogsheads of Virginia tobacco. The Barrowfield Brewery Company offered for sale 'excellent porter, ale and small beer'. A schoolmaster was sought for one of the city's charity schools. Salary £15 per annum. In James Linn's tea and grocery warehouse, King Street, 'best Bohea' cost 2s 4d per pound, 'good fresh Congou' 4s per lb, and 'good Souchong', 5s 6d per lb.

The Lord Provost and magistrates appealed for 'able bodied young men' to complete the quota of Army volunteers raised by the city. Twenty shillings reward was offered for the discovery of Glasgow-born drummer William Hamilton (14), who'd deserted from a recruiting party of the 58th regiment, quartered at Stirling.

Citizens were informed that the stallion 'Young Boffka' was stabled at the Black Bull Inn and prepared to service mares for two guineas 'and half a crown to the groom'. In the village of Meikle Govan, Clyde salmon fishing was let by public roup.

1798   Snaggled Teeth

An 11-year-old girl, employed in a flax mill in Gorbals, was enmeshed in machinery. One of the child's legs was torn off at the knee. With the French allegedly posing a threat to 'freedom', Glaswegians were balloted for service with the Scots Militia. Well-heeled citizens whose names had been drawn sought substitutes to take their places in the ranks, offering inducements of eight to ten guineas. Anyone who failed to report for duty or produce a substitute was liable to be punished as a deserter. Handloom weavers resident in Bridgeton, Calton, and Anderston were among independent-minded working men who ignored the call to arms. Mr Henderson, dentist, Glassford Street, promised to set 'snaggled teeth' straight, providing that the patient was not 'past a certain age'. He also offered to extract teeth from the poor gratis. Messrs Sellars and Dixon sought 'scholars in the polite art of dancing' for their school in Candleriggs. Terms, £1 10s per season. Angus McDonald, Trongate, advertised Jamaica rum at 13s 6d per gallon and 'best gunpowder tea' at 12s per lb.

In the Tontine Tavern, there was let, by public roup, tolls leviable at toll bars on the turnpike roads from Glasgow to Muirkirk, Hamilton, and Eaglesham. 'Four Mule Jeanies, were sold by roup in the spinning-house in Calton. A reward of five guineas was offered for the discovery of schoolmaster John McAulay, Rottenrow, who'd absconded to avoid paying his debts. The wanted man was 'About 5 feet 8 inches high, about 22 years of age, slender made, short black hair, round and smooth faced; wore formerly a chocolate-coloured coat with a black velvet neck, a marseille vest, and thickset breeches. Mr J. Mennon, printer, was Glasgow agent for 'Dr Sibly's Reanimating Solar Tincture', a 'certain cure' for scrofula, scurvy, consumption, gout, rheumatism, piles, rabies, asthma, and many other ailments. Mr Mennon also sold 'Dr Hodson's Parisian Vegetable Syrup ... a safe remedy for all scorbutic and venereal complaints'.

1800   Seditious Hand-Bills

Glasgow Police Commissioners invited tenders for 70 watchmen's sentry boxes, coats, lanterns and rattles. Magistrates urged citizens 'neither to give alms themselves to strolling and public beggars, nor allow their servants to do so'. Trongate Soup Kitchen appealed for donations of potatoes, onions and other vegetables. Baxter's Italian Warehouse, Candleriggs, offered 'reindeer tongues from Russia'.

'Seditious hand-bills', printed by William Paton, Saltmarket, called on Glaswegians to protest against the high price of food. The authorities offered a large reward for Paton's capture: 'smooth-faced, squints a little and stoops somewhat in walking'. In the village of Pollokshaws, citizens – 'much alarmed with appearances of tumult and riot, occasioned by incendiary letters' were enlisted as special constables. Citizens were taxed one guinea for wearing hair powder. 'The poorer sort of clergy' and private soldiers were exempt. Powder-tax dodgers were fined £20.

After a tip-off, Edinburgh police met the Glasgow stagecoach and arrested female shoplifters and pick-pockets making for Auld Reekie's 'Hallow-Fair'. Jonathan Moulton of New Hampshire offered land bargains to Scots 'finding an asylum for the blessings of liberty'.

James Morrison burgled a warehouse – and copped ten years at Botany Bay. 'The Fir Plantation of Easterhouse' was for sale – 'It can be carried to Glasgow by means of the Monkland Canal, at very modest expense'. John Drinnan acquired the 'Anacreonic Tap-Room', Trongate – 'done up in a commodious manner'. The Glasgow Thistle Bank offered £100 reward for information on forgers copying its five-shilling notes.

'The Misses Denoon' opened a school for young ladies – teaching English, French, music, drawing, painting, 'and the other and ornamental parts of Female Education'.

1803   Sharpshooters

The war with France reached a critical stage. 'Patriotic young gentlemen' were invited to enlist in the Glasgow Highland Regiment of Volunteers, familiarly known as 'the Glasgow Sharpshooters' – a new corps raised by the city's Highland Society. Citizens were also urged, 'as men, and as Britons,' to join Anderston and Finnieston Volunteering Corps. The magistrates of Glasgow offered twenty guineas reward for information leading to the detection of a grave robber who'd stolen the corpse of a woman from the Cathedral burying ground. The same amount was offered for information leading to the arrest of an unknown person who'd vandalised one of the town's fire engines.

Mr Moses Gardner, surgeon, 'sign of the Phoenix, No. 283 Gallowgate', informed the public that he had 'just received for sale a considerable quantity of leeches'. Mr McLean, dentist, Argyle Street, offered his services to 'the nobility and gentry' and also advertised 'stumps extracted for the poor from eight till ten every morning *gratis*'. Angus McDonald, Trongate, sold Barclay's Original Ointment, a preparation for venereal disease. ('It does not contain the smallest particle of mercury, or any other dangerous ingredient, and may be safely used by persons of the most delicate constitution.') He also stocked Dr Brodum's Nervous Cordial, Ching's Worm Cakes, Marshall's Orange Soap for the Itch, and MacSparran's Cordial for the Gravel.

The Glasgow Fire Insurance Company offered policies of £300 and upwards. Directors included David Dale, John Stirling, and James Buchanan. In the

Assembly Rooms, Ingram Street, Mr Polito presented a 'grand exhibition of living wonders', including 'a most beautiful leopard'. Ladies and gents, 1s. Working people, servants and children, 6d.

A vacancy arose for a hangman. The previous executioner having been a bad character, the magistrates were 'determined to accept of none but a sober well-behaved man'. The Gorbals Vocal Music Club gave a concert in the Trades' Hall for the benefit of the Royal Infirmary. The brigantine *Glasgow*, Archibald Shandon, master, sailed from Port Dundas to Hamburg. In South Frederick Street, there was exhibited a panorama featuring Napoleon's expedition to Egypt. The Saracen's Lane Foundry, Gallowgate, offered for sale spirit stills and worms.

1805 Nelson Trafalgar

A 'handsome' reward was offered to any able-bodied fellow willing to substitute for a man who'd fallen foul of the Royal Navy press gang, ending up on a ship at Greenock. Elizabeth Boyd – who kept a brothel 'frequented by very young girls' – received 60 days in the Bridewell, the first 30 on bread and water. The authorities sought a 'barbarous mother' who abandoned her baby boy behind a house in Anderston. Jean Craig – 'alias Widow Marsden' – stole cotton yarn from a cart in Briggait. Six months imprisonment, followed by banishment for life.

When news arrived of Nelson's victory at Trafalgar, Anderston Volunteer Corps fired victory volleys in High Street. 'A Glasgow gentleman' offered a guinea to any three sets of parents who christened their sons 'Nelson Trafalgar'.

Domestic servant Janey McWay – contracted to work until 1806 – left her job. 'Measures will be taken for having her punished, with the utmost rigour of law, and as an example to others'. A fiver was offered for information leading to the capture of Andrew Thomson, poacher, accused of shooting partridges on Sir John Maxwell's estate at Newlands. 'Thomson is little more than 20 years of age, rather tall and of a fair complexion, wore a fustian jacket and corduroy breeches; had a game bag under his jacket, carried a double barrelled gun, and hunted with a large, brown and white pointer, very lean.'

George Lumsden discovered three expensive books 'gone missing' from his Argyle Street shop, and requested 'that they be immediately returned'. James Steven, under-miller at Partick Mill, 'embezzled flour' – and was banished for 14 years.

The Olympic Circus, Ingram Street, included child-horseman 'Master Davis' – 'a wonderful phenomenon of juvenile activity' – and a three-year-old child 'in the attitude of Mercury'. 'Bazaget's Oriental Depilatory – celebrated throughout the Eastern nations' was 3/9d a bottle at McDonald's Warehouse, Trongate. McDonald also offered 'Ormskirk's Medicine for the Bite of a Mad Dog'. Daniel Macintosh, labourer, was beaten up near Cowcaddens Toll by five men who robbed him of 15s and threw him into Cracklinghouse Quarry (now Queen Street station), where 'he lay all night unable to move'.

1808   Blue Jamie

Bain & Co ran the 'Mercury' coach between Glasgow and Edinburgh. Inside, 14s, outside, 9s. Persons 'recommended for steadiness and sobriety' were invited to fill vacancies for 'bellmen, or public criers'. Citizens were ordered to 'tie up or confine their dogs', after a 'mad watch dog' bit a man, and a number of dogs, in the vicinity of Broomhouse Toll. James McInabe, better known as 'Blue Jamie', was sent to the Bridewell for three months for defrauding the public by selling 'pepper' composed of 'refuse of mustard'. Residents of Bridgeton were warned to be on the lookout for apprentice Joshua Wyllie, who had done a bunk – 'if he returns to his master, what is past will be forgiven him on his mother's account, as she is in great distress about him'. With the financial backing of the Glasgow Fire Insurance Society, the city was able to send fire engines when required to the outlying villages of Gorbals, Calton, and Anderston. Mrs Alexander opened a boarding and day school for young ladies in George Street. It featured 'an excellent cold bath, supplied with a constant run of fresh water'.

An irate citizen wrote to the press to complain about itinerant door-to-door beggars: ' ... no housekeeper will dispute the inconvenience and irksomeness arising from the continual knocking which these vagrants keep up at their doors; in consequence of which, the half of a servant's time is spent in opening to them'. Ladies who wished to obtain a 'fair complexion, and a clear skin' could purchase 'Mrs Vincent's Celebrated Cowlands Lotion' from David Burton, perfumer, Glassford Street. Mr Burton also stocked 'Solomon's Drops' for the treatment of scurvy, leprosy, scrofula, and gout, and 'Trotter's Oriental Dentifrice, or Asiatic Tooth Powder'. William Harley offered for sale fresh water, piped from his Willow Bank Estate on the Sauchiehall Road. Families taking a full cask for washing purposes were able to take advantage of his special offer – 'Three stoups for a penny'. A reward of 20 guineas was offered for information leading to the arrest of 'evilly disposed persons' who had 'broke near one hundred of the city lamps'.

The managers of the Royal Infirmary launched an appeal for 'linen rags' for use as bandages and dressings. At the Caledonian Tavern, Post Office Close, Trongate, oysters, 'dressed in every variety of sauce', could be obtained 'on the shortest notice'. James Hamilton, grocer, Trongate, advertised 'Adelphi Soda Water ... which has so long been a fashionable beverage in the High Ranks of Society'. Glasgow Dispensary, which extended medical facilities to the poor, celebrated its eighth birthday: 'incurables have not been refused the comfort of an attempt to relieve. This accounts for a large proportion of deaths. In the poor families of soldiers and others, many have recovered.' For the festive season, 'buns, shortbread, and Christmas cakes' were offered for sale in Baxter's Italian Warehouse, Candleriggs.

1810   Illegal Combinations

In 1810, 'persons connected with a Combination ... lately discovered to exist among journeymen cotton spinners' broke windows at mill-owner Henry Houldsworth's Anderston house.

'Instigated by some evil disposed persons connected with the present illegal Combination of the Operative Cotton Spinners against their Masters', a mob of boys tried to torch James Dunlop's cotton mill at Barrowfield. Several spinners were attacked near the mill. Glasgow's Master Cotton Spinners offered substantial rewards to be paid on conviction of the culprits.

A temporary wood structure in Queen Street housed 'the Celebrated Grand Panorama of the Storming of Seringapatam' – consisting of 'nearly three thousand square feet of canvas'. The Olympic Circus offered 'an entirely new Scotch ballet, called Kitty of the Clyde'.

In Bell's Park, Lord Provost James Black laid the foundation stone of William Stark's new lunatic asylum, with great masonic solemnity. William Harley promoted his swimming baths on the 'Sauchy Hall Road'. When the weather is warm, they will be emptied two or three times a week, or oftener if thought necessary'.

Fashionable Glasgow women wore Grecian frocks of 'white Persian gauze'. Hair was *à la Greque*, 'confined with a pearl comb; the curls parted on the forehead by the introduction of a bunch of Persian roses'. Two women colliers were killed at Faskine Colliery 'when ascending the pit by its closing upon them'.

1813   Female Hottentot

Citizens launched an appeal for funds to help 'the inhabitants of the Russian Empire' in the wake of Napoleon's invasion of Russia. A 'grand transparent painting' of the burning of Moscow was exhibited in Candleriggs. Admission 1s. There arose a vacancy for a police officer ('None need apply but such as can write and produce satisfactory certificates of their sobriety and good conduct'). In a tavern in Trongate, 'that most wonderful phenomenon of nature, The Female Hottentot', went on show. Admission 1s 6d. Angus's Academy, Ingram Street, offered 'a morning grammar and elocution class for young ladies'. Police sought the owner of a pig, 'found on one of the public streets of this city'. There was sold, by public roup, spinning machinery 'consisting of a double powered steam engine of four horse power; eight mule carding engines; with roving, drawing and stretching frames; and two mule Jennies of 156 spindles each'.

The Procurator Fiscal offered £5 reward for information on two thieves who had broken out of the Bridewell. One of the men, John Gardner, was 'about five feet five inches in height, stout made, smooth face, pale complexion, fair hair, which he wears combed smooth, light grey eyes, has a shrewd look, and is, in fact, a very shrewd and ingenious rogue'. A judicial investigation was promised after Excisemen shot and killed whisky smugglers on Garscube Road.

'Cheap and pleasant travelling' was promised on the Monkland Canal ('Passengers will be taken in and put out at any place they desire'). Fares: 2s cabin passage; 1s 3d steerage. Police raided 'a rendezvous of thieves and vagabonds' in the High Street. There was offered to let, furnished, a country house, 'pleasantly situated on the Kelvin, nearly two miles from Glasgow, with garden, pleasure ground, and with the use of a neat gig and horse'. In the Assembly Rooms, Ingram Street, 'brilliantly illuminated with transparencies', there was held a 'splendid fancy ball'. Tickets half a guinea each.

1815   British Itch

In 1815, parents dodged free cow pox inoculations for poor children, available at the Surgeon's Hall, St Enoch Square. Clergymen were entreated to tell parishioners about the service. McDonald's Patent Medicine Warehouse, Brunswick Place, sold 'Coxwell's Concrete Lemon Juice', 'Fothergill's Female Pills', 'Senate's Steel Lozenges' and 'British Itch Ointment'. Thomas Stevenson, landlord of Anderston's Museum Tavern, stuffed birds, beasts and reptiles, as a sideline. Prize specimens included a white goat from Russia and a 'two-headed chicken'.

Calton vintner Richard Marshall lost a cow in Stockwell Street. He promised to refund 'all necessary expenses' to the finder. Two days later, Gorbals police found a cow – presumably Marshall's – wandering in Adelphi Street. The Misses Keltie ran a boarding school for young ladies in 'Manhattan Buildings, George Square'.

Elizabeth Greenhorn, collier, was accused of murdering her baby, the body of which had been discovered in the old Monkland pit. 'She absented herself from work at twelve o'clock that day, under pretence of having a headache, and was afterwards found wandering in the pit, almost in a state of insensibility, and having every appearance of recent delivery.' Greenhorn was convicted of concealing pregnancy and sentenced to a month in jail.

'Mr Sadler Jnr' ascended in a balloon from the Grammar School, George Street. Spectators paid 5s a head. He landed at Milngavie. He was only the second person to make a balloon flight from Glasgow. 'A grand panoramic view of the Island of St Helena', where ex-Emperor Napoleon was in exile, was exhibited in a Trongate house.

On December 30, the Clyde rose 17ft above its usual level. Gorbals was flooded. Briggait, Saltmarket, King Street, Stockwell Street and Jamaica Street were under several feet of water.

1817   Pauper Lunatics

A reward of £20 was offered for information leading to the arrest of 'three or four villains' who had committed highway robbery on the road between Pollokshaws and Darnley Toll. A 'great novelty', an 'automaton figure of a tightrope dancer', was exhibited in the Black Bull Inn, Argyle Street. Admission 2s, 1s and 6d. The cells for 'pauper lunatics' in Hutcheson's Hospital were inspected and pronounced 'in good and comfortable order'. The hospital sought subscriptions 'for the relief of the extraordinary poor'. Needy citizens were advised to apply for enrolment as pensioners of the hospital. Applicants had to be at least 50, unless widows with two or more dependent children. A steam engine and power looms were sold by public roup in King Street, Tradeston. Mr Bridges, proprietor of a riding school in York Street, advertised 'Horses broke, for every denomination, on reasonable terms'. A gentleman, returning to Glasgow from Paisley, was severely injured by a 'footpad' and robbed of a large sum of money and a gold watch. William Wade, teacher of elocution, Richmond Street, delivered a course of lectures in 'English Pronunciation'. In the Assembly Rooms, Ingram Street, ladies and gents were taught 'the present mode of Reel Steps, Country Dances, Waltzes, &c.' by Mr Hamilton, dancing master. Charles de Monti, Argyle Street, advertised 'Favourite airs, rondeaux, &c. arranged for the Piano Forte'. The Glasgow Ayrshire Society held a Burns celebration in the Black Bull Inn to mark the Bard's birthday ('dinner on the table precisely at half-past four o'clock').

Shopkeepers in the village of Gorbals were warned to be on the lookout for forged bank tokens. Glasgow residents were told that young boys were entering houses in the town and carrying off silver plate. From one house, 'a complete sweep was made of all the silver articles standing in a sideboard'. 'Indian Jugglers' performed 'extraordinary feats' in the Lyceum Rooms, Nelson Street. Admission 2s and 1s. The Glasgow Female Charity Society organised a procession of 45 girls, whose 'neat and appropriate dress' – dark blue striped gingham frocks, bonnets, white bibs and aprons – met with 'general approbation'. Parents living in the vicinity of Glasgow Cross were warned to be on the alert after 'a woman of mean appearance' decoyed two children into a close in the Old Wynd and removed their clothes. Thieves raided a spirit cellar in St Enoch's Wynd, making off with 'a water stoup full of whisky'.

In the Madeira Court Repository, there was a sale of carriages, curricles, phaetons, tilburies, and gigs. Because 'mad dogs' were loose in Glasgow, citizens were ordered to keep their pets indoors for four weeks. For an attempt on his wife's life, police sought John Gunn, Macalpine Street ('dressed in a blue coat, striped waistcoat on a yellow ground, and grey trowsers'). Finding the dead body of a new-born baby on the banks of the Clyde, near Carlton Place, the authorities of Gorbals offered a reward of five guineas for information leading to the discovery of the 'unnatural mother'. Gregor McGregor and Catherine Jackson were transported for seven years for stealing shirts from a drying green near Dalmarnock.

1820   Gathering Bones

In 1820, Glasgow was gripped by recession. Pawnbrokers did roaring trade. Items pledged included Waterloo medals. Alexander McDonald and Margaret Smith assaulted messenger-at-arms Andrew Wilson in a close in Gallowgate, robbing him of £2 in banknotes and 18s in cash. Both were transported for 14 years. Stuck for funds, Glasgow Royal Infirmary refused admission to 'incurables'.

Two steamboats, *Trusty* and *Industry*, were auctioned at James Montgomery's Steam Boat Tavern, Broomielaw. Gorbals police rescued cotton spinners attacked for working during a strike at Todd and Stevenson's mill, Tradeston. Shopkeepers were warned: 'Villains in the evenings are constantly upon the watch about the doors and windows for an opportunity to dart in upon the unwary shopkeeper.' Three girls, 'who for some time had partly lived by public charity and partly by gathering bones', were found guilty of theft – and banished for seven years.

Soldiers arrested 27 Radical Society delegates 'in full conclave' at a Gallowgate tavern. Sympathisers pelted the troops with stones and 'brick bats'. Gilbert McLeod, printer and editor of a Glasgow Radical paper called *The Spirit of the Union*, appeared at the High Court in Edinburgh. He was found guilty of 'sedition' and transported for five years.

Glasgow's Master Cotton Spinners offered 300 guineas reward for information on 'an armed band of ruffians' who fired several shots into a house in Dale Street, Bridgeton, occupied by men working in John Barr and Co's Greenhead Mill. An attempt was made to set fire to a Milngavie cotton mill with tallow, tar and gunpowder. One arsonist was shot, but they made a successful escape. In Bridgeton, the County Patrol, a rudimentary police force, interrupted a gang burgling a shop. One thief fired a horse pistol, wounding a patrolman. Most of the gang were arrested, including John Sharp – 'a notorious character' – who fired the pistol. James Hunter broke into Paisley Roman Catholic School and stole Bibles, hymn books and tracts. He was transported for 14 years.

Hugh McLean and James Wilson nicked cloth from a Nelson Street shop. Lord Gillies, observing that they were young men, 'fondly hoped they might mend their lives' and 'only' sentenced them to 14 years' transportation. Even less fortunate was Richard Smith, 'aged about sixteen', guilty of house-breaking. The jury recommended mercy, but Gillies sentenced Smith to death by hanging. 'He wept severely and uttered many heavy groans'. John Armstrong, alias Robertson, stole some tools – and was transported for life.

1821   Flying Wardrobe

In 1821, the Dunlop Street Circus featured 'The Flying Wardrobe'. Mr Brown exhibited 'his astonishing Antipodean performances on The Geometrical Ladder and The Masonic Candlestick'. Another performer made a 'Wonderful Ascension from the Back of the Stage to the Gallery, standing on his head on the top of a Real Balloon'. A Gorbals distillery was for sale at £500. An adjacent brewery for £450. Desperate people tried 'Dr Boerhaave's Red Pill – A Mild and Speedy Cure for every stage and symptom of Venereal Disease ... It is especially recommended to those who desire relief without interruption of their ordinary business'. Glaswegians broke into the office at 'Jordanhill Coallery' – and carried off 'an iron safe which would require five or six men to lift'. Their haul was £3 in silver. Near Neilston, excise officers uncovered an illicit distillery – 'carrying on to a large extent'. They destroyed about 500 gallons of wash fermenting in 10 large tuns.

Bridgeton weaver William Lee was accused of inducing a fellow carpet worker to 'go to America and take a machine with him, calculated for the manufacture of carpets on a particular plan, whereby the manufacture of Robert Thomson and Son was very much injured in sale, owing to the introduction of that machinery into New York'. One hundred guineas reward was offered for information leading to the conviction of the murderer of David Robertson, a miner at Govan colliery. Robertson 'was most barbarously murdered on his way from his own house to his work, and his body thrown into a coal pit in the neighbourhood'.

A great auk, caught at St Kilda, escaped from the island of Pladda, off Arran. A reward was offered – two guineas alive, one guinea dead.

1823   Resurrection Men

Body-snatching was on the increase. Citizens armed themselves with pistols and swords to guard the graves of newly-interred relations. While watching beside his sister's grave in a city churchyard, armed with a pistol, a young man was shot dead when the weapon went off by accident. A Bridgeton parent lost two children through illness in one week. On opening the grave of the first child to inter the second, the man discovered that the first cadaver had been stolen by 'resurrection men'. An average of 60 children and adults attended Cowcaddens Educational Society which provided basic literary skills for 'the poorer classes' who otherwise couldn't 'have afforded the means of teaching their children to read'. James Wilson was flogged three times within a month for returning to Glasgow after sentence of banishment had been pronounced. Several months later, the young man was executed for house-breaking. On the scaffold, seconds before his public execution, Wilson embraced the hangman. The stage coach 'Robert Burns' left the Buck's Head Inn daily for London. Inside fare, 112s, outside fare, 61s. The town's Magdalene Asylum advertised for a matron. 'She must be a woman of piety, of prudence, activity, and good temper, and whose character will bear the strictest investigation with regard to correct moral deportment.' Two kind-hearted gents, encountering a young woman and her jailer in the courtyard of the debtors' prison, inquired how much the prisoner owed. The answer was 8s 8d, which the men paid on the spot, securing the girl's discharge. David Wylie, aged about 17, was executed for breaking into a house in Gordon Street. Application was made for commutation of the sentence to transportation, 'but the crime being one of so great enormity, it was deemed absolutely necessary that an example should be made'. Describing the condemned youth's dignified deportment on the scaffold before his public execution, the press commented: 'It is doubtful whether the frequent exhibition of scenes of the above description has not rather a tendency to destroy the moral effects which they are intended to produce.' Public-spirited citizens launched a fund to preserve 'liberty of access along the banks of the Clyde'. Police patrols were strengthened for the duration of the Glasgow Fair, and special constables were instructed to 'mingle with the throng' in order to detect delinquents. Two city tea merchants were each fined £20 for adulterating their merchandise with 'peat moss'. A 'gentleman' was robbed of a considerable sum of money in 'an irregular house' in Bell Street. Two girls were apprehended and the money recovered. The brig *Ann* sailed from Glasgow Harbour to Quebec.

The steamboat *Comet* sailed from the Broomielaw to Fort William. In the City Bazaar, Candleriggs, pigeons cost 10d and 12d a pair and eggs sold for 7d and 8d a dozen. Findlay, Connal & Co, brokers, Virginia Street, announced 'public sale of buffalo hides'. The Rev Dr Macgill preached a sermon in aid of a fund to buy improving religious books for the prison library.

1826   Light-Fingered Gentry

In 1826, city businessmen launched a relief fund for starving victims of recession. The Dean of Guild pointed out that, unlike in 1816 and 1819, when there was political unrest, the poor were now supine and 'bowed with submission to whatever was proposed for their relief'. Weavers quarried stone for road works. 'Mr Gardner, perfumer, hair cutter and patent peruke maker', owner of 'the Emporium of Fashion', Queen Street, offered 'a choice assortment of French and German hair ... in the newest and most approved style of fashion'. 'Monsieur Boulogne's French Dancing Academy', Queen Street, taught 'much admired six-drilles, as danced by the Noblesse in the French capital'. Andrew Liddell & Co, Argyle Street, advertised 'portable water closets'.

George Wombell's Circus – 'thirteen wagons literally crammed with wild animals' – included lions Nero and Wallace. 'Thousands hourly visit Nero in his den, and depart highly gratified having been locked up in the cage with a wild beast!'

Parliament abolished the National Lottery, in existence for 150 years. The final draw had six top prizes of £30,000. Promenading in the privately owned Botanic Gardens, Sauchiehall Road (west of what is now Charing Cross), gentry were entertained by the band of the Lancers, playing 'exhilarating marches, quadrilles and waltzes'. Alexander McKenzie was jailed for 12 months for stealing a silver watch from the cabin of a schooner at Port Dundas. Known thief Jean Livingston copped 14 years' transportation for filching a pocket book containing £15 from Neil Walker in a Trongate tavern.

Isaac Baxter, Candleriggs, stocked 'Cheltenham, Harrogate and Leamington Salts', along with an opiate called 'Lancaster Black Drop'. James Wallace, High Street and Gallowgate, sold '11 per cent over-proof malt whisky', at 6/8d per gallon. 'Mr Meek', Miller Street, offered 'Atkinson's Bear Grease for the Hair'.

Offers were invited for the Hillhead coal mine, 'situated in the immediate neighbourhood of Glasgow and the village of Partick'. City pavements were so dirty that 'Each citizen's pantaloons and the tail of his coat require half an hour's brushing every morning, which forms a wear equal to two months' actual service.' Ayr Horse Fair was 'attended by a detachment of light-fingered gentry from Glasgow, which operated with considerable success on the pockets of several individuals in the market, and effected a safe retreat in two divisions by the Glasgow coach'.

A tipsy 'young gentleman' had an overnight stay in the police office, during which fellow prisoners relieved him of a gold eyeglass, a purse containing £3, a silk handkerchief, a snuffbox, and two gold seals. A man was killed when he climbed a wall in Queen Street and fell into the Cracklinghouse Quarry. Two women, 'seen lurking about the Cathcart Road, near Crosshill', were stopped and searched. They had two bags containing 'thirteen fowls with their necks drawn and apparently new killed'.

1828   Hue and Cry!

City magistrates published a 'Hue and Cry!', offering a reward of 20 guineas for information leading to the arrest of Neil Arnot, whose wife had been murdered in a house in Drygate. A record crowd, estimated 'as high as fifty thousand', witnessed the public execution of Bell McMenemy and Thomas Connor for the crime of assault and robbery. The huge turnout was attributed to the fact that it was 35 years since a woman had been executed in Glasgow. Body-snatchers made off with the corpse of an old woman who'd expired in a lodging house in Calton.

A young medical student was chased through the streets by an angry crowd after he was seen leaving a house in Saltmarket with a stillborn baby under his greatcoat. Gravedigger William Robertson was sent to the Bridewell for 60 days for stealing the teeth from the corpse of a woman who'd died of fever in the Royal Infirmary. Teeth taken from corpses were disposed of to manufacturers of false teeth. Henry Gillies was sent to the Bridewell for nine months for stealing the body of an elderly woman from Anderston churchyard. In Anderston, a 15-month-old baby died after being given whisky at a New Year party. A tavern keeper in Saltmarket was fined £5 for selling whisky to four young lads, one of whom was carried unconscious to the police office. An Irishman, newly arrived in town, was taken into a house in Gallowgate by 'a profligate female', plied with whisky, and robbed of 59 gold sovereigns. After 'repeated complaints' by shopkeepers in Bell Street and High Street, between 30 and 40 'disorderly females' were rounded up by the police. City apothecaries stocked 'Butler's Cooling Aperient Powder' for indigestion, 'Inglish's Scots Pills' for gout, and 'Dr Buchan's Domestic Female Pill, for Complaints Peculiar to the Female Sex'.

Citizens flocked to the Trades House, Glassford Street, to gawk at 'Two Chinese Ladies, the only female natives of the Chinese Empire ever seen in Europe'. Admission 1s. A reward of 30 guineas was offered for information leading to the apprehension of three young men who'd broken out of the town's gaol. Acting on information received, police arrested the men in a secluded cottage on rural Sauchiehall Road. The proprietor of The Milton Tavern, Saltmarket, advertised 'accommodation for travellers arriving by the night coaches'. Citizens were warned to be on their guard against 'the insidious tricks of that fraternity of vagabonds known by the title of "ring-droppers".' The sloop *Agnes* sailed from the Broomielaw to Rotterdam. Elizabeth McLain was transported for seven years for pinching a piece of printed cotton from a warehouse in Candleriggs. Parish authorities offered a reward of £5 5s for the detection of individuals abandoning unwanted babies in Tradeston, Lauriston, and Hutchesontown. The Glasgow City Mission employed ten urban missionaries, 'visiting the abodes of the poor, and instructing the ignorant in the various doctrines of Christianity'.

In Anderson's University, Dr Spurzheim delivered a series of lectures on the fashionable 'science' of phrenology. Drummond & Corbet, Saltmarket Street, advertised 'a choice assortment of Bombazeens and general Family Mourning'. A working model of a 'patent steam carriage' was exhibited in the Black Bull Inn, Argyle Street. Admission 1s.

1830   Loose Women

Clyde-caught salmon went for 1/6d per lb. 'Mr Morgan' opened a 'London-style chop house' in London Road. Attractions included hot and cold showers. From weaving shops in Finnieston and Calton, thieves stole plaids and shawls from the looms. Walking from Kirkintilloch to Glasgow, a weaver was set upon by a gang of muggers, who beat him up and escaped with £4 10s.

A boy – 'about 10 years of age' – was jailed for 60 days for pinching two books from a shop. Glasgow miners demanded wage increases from 3s to 4s a day. The Theatre Royal, Dunlop Street, featured 'Mademoiselle D'Jeck, the colossal elephant'. An elderly man appeared in court, 'surrounded by a legion of loose women'. Accused of 'keeping a disorderly brothel near Glasgow Cross', he was jailed for 60 days. Catherine McGillivray was transported for seven years for stealing a milk pitcher. 'A respectable young girl' was enticed into a close in Stockwell Street and stripped of her shoes. Such robberies were 'of frequent occurrence'.

'Mr Green the celebrated English aeronaut' – the third person to ascend in a balloon from Glasgow – took off from the Cattle Market, Gallowgate. His ascent was witnessed by 'countless multitudes'. He landed at Uddingston. Cotton spinners demanded cessation of the infamous 'truck' system, whereby employers compelled workers to take goods from company stores, in lieu of wages. A householder in 'the peaceful village of Baillieston' found 'a fine female child, about four days old' on her doorstep. The Old Monkland Parish Session allowed 4s a week for the infant's maintenance.

Two 'rather good looking young men', John Hill and William Porter, assaulted an elderly man in Townhead, robbing him of 7s. After they'd been sentenced to death, 'Porter turned round to his companion in crime and kissed him'. For stealing linen shirts from Gorbals tollhouse, Daniel McDonald, 'being by habit and repute a thief', copped 14 years' transportation. James Durham, who'd 'already served five years aboard the hulks', received 14 years' transportation for stealing clothes from an Anderston house.

Two suspected body-snatchers, arrested in Cowcaddens, narrowly escaped with their lives when they were attacked by an angry crowd. One ran into a house and escaped by the back door. The other was 'dreadfully abused by the crowd'. Using a duplicate key, body-snatchers gained access to a locked 'mort-safe' in Shettleston churchyard and removed the corpse of a young girl.

The driver of a Glasgow 'noddy' – a hackney carriage – was charged with 'furious driving' while drunk. His noddy demolished a lamppost. Fined £5. The Glasgow and West of Scotland Temperance Society, under the aegis of publisher William Collins, opened a temperance coffee house. Coffee was much cheaper than tea. William McEwan & Sons, Trongate, sold 'Fine Mocha' at 2/4d per lb. Booksellers offered a volume of beauty hints 'by a Lady of Distinction', which 'may, with safety and advantage, be put into the hands of a young lady'.

1833   Wonderful Liberalism

In 1833, a little boy, 'not more than four years old', was sold to a High Street chimney sweep – for ten bob. James McEwan (9) stole a tankard from a pub. 'His stepmother was a worthless character, who daily sent him to the streets to beg.' He'd been 'found at midnight at least 10 times, starving with cold and hunger'.

On January 1, a young man, entering a close in Stockwell Street, fell on his Ne'erday bottle, which broke and wounded him so severely that he subsequently died. During the festive season, citizens were serenaded by the 'City Waits' – 'bereft of sight, of unexceptionable moral character, and the most of them burthened with large families'. A little girl 'fell into convulsions' and died after being given strong drink 'in honour of the season'.

Panic ensued when cholera struck the village of Thornwood, west of Partick, 'in one week taking off four out of seven cases'. Nearly 100 villagers fled. Mary MacShaffray, cotton-stretcher, Calton, was entering the close of her house when several men – 'members of a Combination' – threw 'vitriol' (strong sulphuric acid) into her face. The authorities offered 100 guineas reward for information leading to convictions. Cotton bosses opposed the Factory Act, designed to reduce the working day to 10 hours. Glasgow mill workers worked 12-hour shifts, five days a week, with a nine-hour shift on Saturdays.

In Townhead, two engineers, described as '"nobs", or workmen who do not comply with the regulations of the Trades Unions', were 'hooted at, bespattered with mud, and jostled' by 'mechanics and labourers'. They were said to earn 18 bob a week. At Glasgow's Water Bailie Court, a practical joker was fined 10/6d for 'handing a cigar charged with gunpowder to a person in a steamboat'. Building in Glasgow was 'brisk'. Masons' wages had been static for five years – at 2s a day in winter and 2/6d a day in summer.

'Sacrilegious thieving' was increasing. Citizens were advised not to leave Bibles and psalm books lying around in churches. *The Glasgow Courier* blamed 'this age of wonderful liberalism'. Thieves robbed a shop in a four-storey tenement in Stockwell Street by coming down the chimney flue. Several sweeps were arrested. Henry Burnet (26) was executed for assault and robbery. He had previously 'spent five years of his ill-fated life on board the hulks'.

Bridgeton villagers complained about the lack of a local police force. 'The streets present a most disgraceful appearance, being the perpetual scenes of drunkenness and disorder.' When fire broke out in a Candleriggs shop which stocked radical newspapers, *The Glasgow Courier* described the incident as 'almost a God's providence'. A Glasgow gentleman, 'possessing an ample income, of character and of family irreproachable', sought a wife – 'her fortune not less than ten thousand pounds'.

'Herr Ruby Jourdain', dental surgeon, Renfield Street, offered 'Incorrodible mineral teeth, without wires, springs or any other ligatures' – £20 a set. Miss Helen Stevens – a 'dashing young lady' – kept 'a house of bad fame' in Bell Street. Sixty days' imprisonment. During Glasgow Fair, police rounded up 'bad characters found loitering about the town in order that the inhabitants might enjoy themselves in security'.

'Sanderson's Fly Boats' plied every weekday night on the Forth and Clyde Canal, between Edinburgh and Port Dundas. The journey took more than seven hours. 'Passenger steam carriages' of the Garnskirk and Glasgow Railway left St Rollox for Airdrie four times daily.

In a Bell Street restaurant, two girls engaged a farmer in conversation and relieved him of a valuable silver watch. One was 'a most experienced thief, particularly on market days, among the gash folks from the country'. 'A man of colour' – newly arrived in Glasgow from New York – sought a position as a 'steward, coachman or body servant'.

'Dr Boerhaave's Celebrated Red Pill' – 4/6d a box – was 'famous for the cure of every stage and symptom of a Certain Complaint'.

1836   Learned Pig

In 1836, 'a very interesting-looking young woman' tried to drown herself in the Clyde. She was unemployed, behind with her rent and had been evicted from her lodgings. A boy (4) was abducted from Adelphi Street, Gorbals, 'by one of those abandoned females who go about stripping children of their clothes'. Anne Spalding got 60 days for stealing horsehair stuffing from the seats of hackney cabs. Destitute Irish people besieged Glasgow's police office. '£50 a day would not be enough to pay the passage of those who wish to return home, and cannot find the means'. William Waugh, a little boy 'by habit and repute a thief', was convicted of house-breaking and transported for seven years. The same sentence was imposed on another small boy, John Murphy. He sighed and said: 'It'll wear awa'.

Charged with stealing a 56lb weight from a plumber's shop, a woman claimed it had been 'thrown into her lap' by another woman as she was innocently passing along the street. Glasgow police sought the owners of a brown and white spotted cow and a black goat. Between 30 and 40 'abandoned females' were charged with being 'street pests' in the vicinity of High Street and Bell Street. At 'Mr Gullan's Academy', George Square, 'young ladies' were taught 'grammar and composition, geography, and the use of the Globes'.

A brothel-keeper was jugged for being accessory to a theft from 'a simple-looking Hibernian'. Glasgow Fair attractions included the 'Hottentot Venus' and 'Toby, the learned pig'. 'Mr Cooke's Royal Circus', Saltmarket, featured 'The Revolt of the Harem, or the Sultan's Pastime'. For one night only, 'a real fox chase' took place in the Circus. The Glasgow Necropolis was 'now the first place to which everyone thinks of conducting a stranger'. 'A countryman' encountered 'miscreant ring-droppers' on a steamboat en route for Broomielaw. On arrival, he was decoyed to Glasgow Green and 'swindled out of £22 for some gewgaws which would hardly have excited the cupidity of an inhabitant of the Sandwich Islands'.

'Poor emaciated females, with infants in their arms and little ones at their feet in plenty', were charged 'with being vagrants and asking alms'. One woman told how, after her husband became ill, she 'had sold every article in their lodgings for his and their children's support ... there not being a mouthful of bread in the house to give either her sick husband or her starving children, she had come to the streets for the first time in her life, if almost in desperation'. A young Paisley woman 'of fashionable appearance' swindled Glasgow shopkeepers. Sixty days' hard labour – on bread and water. Another woman, 'said to be from Paisley, of good exterior', absconded with the child of a fellow lodger.

1839   326 Hankies

In 1839, between February 9 and February 15, Glasgow's Night Asylum for the Houseless, St Enoch's Wynd, gave temporary shelter to 632 persons: 117 men, 272 women, 124 boys and 118 girls. Directors promised that neither 'door-to-door beggars' nor 'loose women' would be admitted. Ships left Broomielaw for Bombay, Calcutta, Jamaica, Havana, Malta, Quebec, Montreal, Rio de Janeiro, Singapore and New South Wales. It was possible to sail to Rotterdam from Port Dundas.

Police found three destitute children, the youngest about four, wandering the streets 'in the most abject wretchedness and poverty'. They were delivered to the Barony Poorhouse. Female Chartists met in the Methodist Chapel, Spreull's Court, Trongate. Most of the 60 or 70 women present were from Bridgeton. A 'sturdy beggar' got 60 days in prison. His daughter (4), who'd 'lain out in the cold to the danger of her life', was sent to the 'pauper hospital'. Thieves broke into a Buchanan Street warehouse. Police retrieved a bag containing 326 silk handkerchiefs.

Footpads held up a gentleman on Glasgow Green and at pistol point robbed him of 7s. One of the robbers apologised, explaining he'd been driven to crime 'by want of employment'. In its first year, the 'House of Refuge' for juvenile delinquents admitted more than 200 boys, who'd been 'wandering in rags about the streets by day, sleeping on cold stairs by night'. In Finnieston, preachers addressed large crowds 'deeply concerned about the state of their souls'. Robert Owen lectured in the 'Hall of Science', Trongate. His followers were described as 'Socialists'. City swells relaxed at 'Paul Spencer's Cigar Salon', Hutcheson Street, during 'evening harmonic meetings' featuring 'a first-rate vocalist and performer on the pianoforte'.

Gorbals police arrested a gang of female house-breakers. 'Mr Batty's Circus Royal', Hope Street, was destroyed by fire. Sir Walter Scott had been present at a previous performance, when 'Mr Price made no less than 40 evolutions in the air with his body, much after the manner and with the celerity, of a steam-engine fly-wheel'.

Marshall's New Panorama, Buchanan Street – 'lighted with gas' – depicted Grace Darling and her father rescuing survivors from the wreck of the steamer *Forfarshire*.

1842   Chain-Droppers

Typhus fever was reported to be rife in 'the low wynds and dirty streets and courts' of the old town. 'Likenesses of Undeviating Accuracy' were 'cut in a few seconds' at the Hubard Gallery, 74 Queen Street. When arrested in London Street,

Thomas and Alexander Muir, described as 'notorious chain-droppers', sported gold watches and chains, gold finger rings, silver-headed canes, and emerald breast pins. The men had achieved notoriety by working a scam to defraud Irishmen newly arrived in Glasgow. An Anderston woman's baby died after being given neat whisky as 'medicine'. James Galloway, described as 'an old offender', was apprehended in Jamaica Street with 20 stolen bibles and psalm books in his possession. In the City Hall, there was held 'a grand concert for the benefit of the Asylum for the Houseless Poor'. William Mitchison, Buchanan Street, offered for sale 'Gems of the Ballroom, a Collection of Popular Waltzes'. In St George's Church, the Reverend Dr Muir preached the annual sermon in aid of the Old Man's Friend Society.

Ships sailed from the Broomielaw to Demerara, Trinidad, and Madras. Reporting an increase in the number of beggars, the press fulminated: 'Begging is not the wretched trade that many have supposed. Those who are maimed, or can exhibit disgusting sores to excite the commiseration of the public admit that they can earn from 3s to 4s per day'. Several pauper inmates of the House of Industry for Females, St Enoch's Wynd, were sent to prison for 20 days for selling their petticoats, property of the institution, to purchase drink. On 12th July, police ordered the removal of Orange insignia from a building in Gallowgate. The press reported: 'These party displays are extremely liable to irritate and excite the Roman Catholic part of the population to retaliation'. Sarah Moonie, convicted of trying to pass a forged 6d in a shop in Clyde Street, Anderston, was sentenced to seven years' transportation. At a crowded meeting in the City Hall, there were clashes between Chartists and 'complete suffragists'.

Three sheep, belonging to Mr Veitch, flesher, were stolen from Glasgow Green. The offals were later discovered in the Fleshers' Haugh. The Glasgow, Paisley, Kilmarnock, and Ayr Railway advertised pleasure excursions to Ayr. Third class, 3s return. A woman named Curly, keeper of a 'wee pawn' in Prince's Street, was sent to the Bridewell for 60 days for resetting articles stolen by three young boys. The press commented: 'the existence of these "wee pawns", or low brokers' shops, is productive of a greater amount of petty theft than all other causes put together, from the facilities which they afford for the disposal of stolen property'. Spirit merchants Robert Park & Co, Gallowgate, advertised malt whisky at 7s 2d per gallon.

1844 Pantechnetheca

A 'Hydropathic Soirée' took place in the Trades' Hall, Glassford Street. Paupers in the Town's Hospital, Clyde Street, received a special Ne'erday treat of hot pies, bread and cheese, and ale. From January 6 to January 12, 595 people – including 37 boys and 58 girls – sheltered in the Night Asylum for the Houseless. *The Glasgow Courier* railed: 'It is not uncommon now to have whole families ranged along the streets – the husband and wife in clean and decent clothes, the children in night-caps as white as snow, and all of them wearing looks of plaintiveness which could not be better portrayed on the stage.'

Violet Dailly – 'gaily dressed' – copped 60 days for brothel-keeping – and was conveyed to jail in 'Howard', the town's new police vehicle. Two boys smashed a Trongate jeweller's window and nicked a dozen gold rings. 'The City and Bay of New York' was the subject of a 'Diorama' at the Monteith Rooms, Buchanan Street … 'so correctly got up that those who have been in New York can point out not only the street where they resided, but the identical house'. Messrs Kevan and Buttle, Argyle Street, offered 'Ladies' Musquash Riding Boas'.

Mary Boyle – 'in appearance a gentle and interesting girl about 16 years of age' – was transported for 10 years for house-breaking. 'She broke into a torrent of the foulest blasphemy and abuse which, perhaps, was ever heard in the Glasgow Court House.' 'One of the class of unfortunates' threw herself into the Clyde after being 'struck and abused' in an Old Wynd lodging house. She was saved by Mr Geddes of the Humane Society. 'Numbers of people' poached salmon between Dalmarnock Bridge and Carmyle Mills. Leading citizens promoted 'public baths for the working classes'. 'Bathing has an excellent moral effect by preventing the craving for unnecessary stimulants.'

'Miss McCallum', West Nile Street, sold 'The Patent Automatic Calculator ... performing both addition and subtraction of any sum from one farthing to one million pounds'. 'General Tom Thumb – The American Man in Miniature', 13 years old and 25 inches high, appeared at the City Hall, wearing Highland dress and Napoleonic costume. At the Theatre Royal, Fanny Ternan (8) – 'The Celebrated Infant Prodigy' – attracted large audiences. In Bridgeton, robberies were 'almost of nightly occurrence'. 'Mr Hyman's Pantechnetheca', Argyle Street, offered 'Ladies' Riding Habits' and servants' liveries.

Drivers of horse-drawn 'minibuses' were accused of dangerous driving. At

Broomielaw, a minibus made 'a complete tumble heels over head, a wheel flying off one way and the driver another'. Drivers 'charged an exorbitantly as they pleased'. Mr E J Pickering offered daguerreotype photographic portraits 'without the agency of the sun'. 'Child-stripping' was becoming more common. Stolen clothing ended up in 'wee pawns' in Trongate. A little girl, stolen from Camlachie, was recovered in Liverpool.

Police broke up a fight in Havannah Street, and were attacked by 'the rascally multitude'. 'Coiners' were caught in a house in Old Vennel, with £1 worth of coins in their possession – 'all base but shining bright, and apparently just new from the moulds'.

A Liverpudlian – 'dressed in the very pink of fashion' – was charged with picking a lady's pocket in Buchanan Street. Enticed into an Old Wynd brothel, a collier was pied with 'porter infused with snuff' and robbed of his watch. Railways provided thieves with rich pickings. 'A gentleman', travelling first-class from Edinburgh to Glasgow, had his expensive gold cravat pin filched when the train entered the tunnel at Queen Street. Four times daily, James Walker ran a 6d omnibus from Trongate to Botanic Gardens. There, promenades, enlivened with military bands, were 'a specimen of recreation in a great measure new to the bulk of our citizens'.

1846   Pedestrianism

'Pedestrianism' was becoming a popular sport. A Glasgow compositor named Elder won several sovereigns in a wager, walking 60 miles in 15 hours. In a confrontation with squaddies at the foot of Saltmarket Street, police officers and watchmen were assaulted with stones, sticks, and army belts. After several hundred university students went on the rampage in the vicinity of the Old College in High Street, ten of the young gents were each fined two guineas for breaking street lamps and assaulting police constables. The court dealt less leniently with Joseph Scott, found guilty of stealing a woollen cravat from a shop door in High Street, and sent to prison for 10 months. A female pawnbroker of foreign extraction was fined a guinea for 'profaning the Sabbath' by carrying on business in a 'wee pawn' in Prince's Street, near Glasgow Cross. The court heard that the poor of the district were only allowed to pledge articles on condition that they purchased provisions at high prices from the pawnbroker. Members of the Glasgow Emancipation Society met in the City Hall to hear a lecture by Frederick Douglas, 'a self-liberated American slave'.

Samuel McLachlan, an old man 'who obtained a precarious living as a bone-gatherer', fell down in a close in High Street and expired. The dead man left a widow and child 'entirely destitute'. Condemning the 'influx of Irish', the press railed: 'It would be well that our Irish friends should understand that the City of Glasgow is at present overrun with poor, and that by flocking hither in droves they are only exposing themselves to certain misery'. At the Glasgow Fair, the city's privately-owned Royal Botanic Gardens were thrown open to the working classes. The latter were reminded that 'they will have an opportunity of not only justifying the confidence reposed in them on this occasion, but of showing by their good conduct that the working classes of Glasgow may be safely admitted to any exhibition either of nature or of art'. Among the attractions laid on in the Gardens for pukka West Enders were promenade concerts featuring 'Ethiopian Serenaders'.

Mr Cohen, Buchanan Street, advertised 'spheroidal crystalline lenses'. Steel frames, 10s to 12s; gold frames, 30s to 40s. W Gardner, Royal Bank Place, advertised 'Daguerreotype portraits' from 8s to 30s; coloured, 2s 6d extra. In fashionable Norfolk Street, Gorbals, a little girl was robbed of a pair of 'handsome new cloth galoshed boots'. Parents, already worried about 'child-strippers', were warned that thieves were also engaged in 'the nefarious practice of cutting off the graceful ringlets and plats of hair from children who happen to be out of doors unattended'. William Abbott & Co operated a twice-daily omnibus service from Trongate to Canniesburn, via Maryhill.

In the populous industrial suburb of Bridgeton, where there was no police force, it was reported that petty crime was flourishing: 'people have been taken into houses the worse for liquor, and their clothes stripped off and pawned – children, sent messages by their parents, have had their baskets and all the contents carried off – and Sunday, being the day when there is most leisure, is taken up by the blackguard youngsters playing at handball, and other games.'

1848   Fine Bodies

In 1848, legions of unemployed Glaswegians depended on soup kitchens. Huge crowds gathered on Glasgow Green. Harangued by Chartists, part of the multitude marched on the city's East End gas works to cut off the city's supply. Others smashed plate glass windows in exclusive Buchanan Street. Firearms were removed from gunsmiths' shops. In Bridgeton, the gas works contingent was met by the 'Enrolled Pensioners', a corps of elderly ex-soldiers. The Pensioners – some sporting Waterloo medals – charged with bayonets, but couldn't disperse the mob. The veterans fired volleys at point-blank range. David Carruth, a weaver, was shot dead. Several others were wounded.

'Numerous and fine bodies of young gentlemen' enrolled as special constables. Engineering boss Robert Napier volunteered hundreds of his employees as special constables. The Duke of Hamilton offered to call out the Yeoman Cavalry. 'When the illustrious of the land as well as the industrious and honest mechanic are joined in the same good cause, we have no fear that it will soon be again as it should be.'

The 'Diorama', West Nile Street, featured a 'Swiss village' with 'realistic atmospheric effects'.

1850   City Arabs

A new 'Ragged School' – 'a neat castellated structure' – was being erected in Rottenrow. It was designed to accommodate hundreds of destitute children, described as 'the arabs of the city'. A 'fruit soirée' was held in the Merchants' Hall, Hutcheson Street, under the auspices of the Scottish Temperance League. 'Sabbath profanation' worried the authorities. Worst offenders were tavern-keepers and small shopkeepers. At Anderston police court, a man was fined ten bob for playing pitch and toss on the Sabbath, near Garscube Road.

At Calton police court, Thomas Haggarty, flesher, was fined ten bob also – for keeping a ferocious dog 'for fighting purposes'. 'Hundreds of dogs are trained in Glasgow to worry and kill their species ... dog fights are a frequent source of amusement, and even of profit, to no inconsiderable number of the lowest classes.' Wombell's Menagerie mourned the untimely demise of its finest specimen – a rhinoceros, valued at 1000 guineas.

The AGM of the Industrial Schools Association heard that 'a large number of the destitute children who infest the streets of this city prefer being sent to jail rather than go to the House of Refuge'. Andrew Kyle, aged 'about six or seven ... so diminutive that his head could not be seen over the bar', stole 3lbs of butter from a Stockwell Street shop. He refused to go to the House of Refuge in Duke Street. Sixty days' imprisonment.

Police raided 'an establishment of a certain character in Trongate' and found two elderly gentlemen playing cards and enjoying 'a familiar tête-à-tête with two showily-dressed females named Louisa Fitzcharles and Ann Wilson'. The women were fined £5 – which they 'paid readily'.

Police also stopped a bare-knuckle prizefight near Rutherglen Bridge. 'The combatants bore evident marks of having received a fearful punishment, their faces being much cut, swollen, and disfigured.' Ann Meek, frequently fined for keeping a 'disorderly house' in Jamaica Street, tried to commit suicide by jumping into the Clyde. Two babies, 'comfortably wrapped in a tartan shawl', were abandoned outside the Roman Catholic chapel in Clyde Street. A woman was charged with throwing her baby into the Paisley canal. She told a court she'd been deserted by her husband and was destitute. The infant survived.

On display at the Trades' Hall, Glassford Street, was a 'Panorama of the Mississippi – upwards of three thousand miles of scenery ... represented on three miles of canvas'. The screw steamer *City of Glasgow* sailed regularly from Glasgow to New York. A cabin passage cost 20 guineas.

1851   Low Immorality

Glasgow's Night Asylum for the Houseless contained a nightly average of 77 persons, as opposed to 92 in 1849 and 126 in 1848. This was due to 'the improved circumstances of the poor, from work being easier obtained, and from the comparative low price of food'.

Glasgow's annual Regatta, near Glasgow Green, was 'an amusement which partakes not in the slightest degree of the low immorality of show-booths'. Gorbals Juvenile Abstinence Society enjoyed a trip to Ballochmyle.

Catherine Matthews, 'a fraudulent pauper', obtained five bob from the city's pauper hospital by pretending that her husband had deserted her. A Gorbals man 'stripped off and pawned for whisky the clothes which his two little motherless girls had received from the Industrial or Ragged Schools'. A shoemaker copped 30 days 'for docking the tails of several cows and stealing the hair'.

'Temperance trips' to London's Crystal Palace and Great Exhibition were available on the crew steamer *European*, commanded by Captain McCallum – 'a staunch abstainer'. The voyage took 73 hours and cost £3 5s. Four days were allowed for sightseeing. Passengers slept on board, saving on hotels. A third-class rail return between Glasgow and London cost £2.

An explosion in the Victoria pit, Nitshill, killed more than 60 miners, including a number of young boys. The pit, belonging to Messrs Coats, had been 'ventilated on the most admirable principles'. A scale model of the mine was about to be exhibited at the Great Exhibition when the disaster occurred. Rescuers tunnelled in search of survivors. 'Women stood in little groups, with faces swollen with weeping, and most silent from the very exhaustion of grief and despair'.

A woman in her thirties took lodgings in Broomielaw Street, locked her bedroom door, and killed herself with laudanum. Police forced entry to a Marlborough Street house and discovered crucibles, moulds for casting pennies, and 'all the apparatus for coining on a large scale'. Dud pennies sold at 30 shillings' worth for £1 to hawkers and small traders who 'got rid of them in retail transactions with the lower orders'.

1853　　Ungrateful Paupers

Glasgow stonemasons were reported to be 'wearing mustachios as a preventive against the injury done to the system by fine particles of sand [pneumoconiosis] while they are engaged in dressing stones'. Citizens went in fear of 'garrotting' – mugging by strangulation – a recurring moral panic of the period. The *Reformer's Gazette* alleged: 'Scarcely a day or night passes over without some startling account of the cool and deliberate perpetration of this crime in Glasgow.' A prosperous merchant was 'decoyed' into a close in St George's Place by 'a disreputable female', who relieved him of a silver watch and items of jewellery. Detectives traced the woman to a hovel in High Street. She was sent to the Bridewell for 60 days, with hard labour. While watching a public execution in Jail Square, three spectators had their watches pinched. William Ward, who filched a silk handkerchief from a passer-by in Candleriggs Street, got nine months' chokey. Gorbals Parochial Board advertised for an Inspector of Poor. Salary £100 per annum. City magistrates refused to renew the licences of 'wee pawnbrokers' convicted of resetting stolen goods. Stolen property, including clothes stripped from children, often ended up in 'wee pawns' in the neighbourhood of Glasgow Cross. Magistrates also clamped down on street beggars, described as 'professional female mendicants with hired babies'. The press raged: 'The giving of doles to people of this class is only perpetuating the mischief, and fostering a race of impostors.' Two frail old women, described as 'ungrateful paupers', went to prison for 30 days for being drunk and disorderly in the town's poorhouse. For swiping a silk handkerchief from the pocket of a gentleman, a young lad named McKinnoch, described as 'an incorrigible pickpocket', was sentenced to 25 strokes of the birch and 30 days in the Bridewell. Another youngster, William Beattie, was transported for seven years for the theft of a silver-plated candlestick from a shop in Bridgegate Street. Mary Dunn copped the same sentence for stealing £105 in notes from the house of fur merchant Levi Metzenburgh, Stockwell Street. Margaret McGuire, found guilty of stealing three petticoats from a house in King Street, was also transported for seven years.

There was offered to let, at Garnet Hill, 'a parlour and bedroom, with the use of plunge and shower bath'. Rent 9s per week. Citizens flocked to the Theatre Royal for a dramatised version of *Uncle Tom's Cabin*. When Mrs Beecher Stowe arrived in Glasgow from the USA, the city's Anti Slavery Committee held a soirée in the City Hall in her honour. Clippers and brigs sailed regularly from Glasgow Harbour to Melbourne. Messrs Neilson & McIntosh, Stockwell Street, advertised passages to Australia for £20 and £30. John Dobie, Argyle Street, advertised 'a large stock of revolvers and other pistols' for use in Australia. Thomas Elder, Duke Street, offered for sale 'portable iron houses' suitable for 'parties about to emigrate to Australia'. Alexander Cross & Sons, Argyle Street, were agents for 'the genuine Peruvian Guano'. A female teacher was required for a school in Black Boy Close, Gallowgate. Salary £20 per annum.

1855   Dog's Close

The Crimean War was raging. Glasgow men were serving with the 42nd Regiment of the Highland Brigade. In the Theatre Royal, Dunlop Street, the Battle of Alma was re-enacted as 'a brilliant military spectacle', attracting 'the rank and fashion of the city'.

Pick-pockets operated on omnibuses, railway platforms and steamboats. Gangs of card sharpers made regular rail excursions to fleece unsuspecting travellers. Thirty to sixty days' imprisonment was the usual sentence for wife beaters. Robert Dyer was sentenced to 60 days' hard labour for a brutal assault on his wife, who lost the sight of an eye. Thomas Gardner or Garven (8) – already well known to the police as a rogue and vagabond – tried to pick ladies' pockets at Broomielaw steamboat wharf. Sixty days' imprisonment and five years in Reformatory School.

The Forbes Mackenzie Act, which closed Scotland's pubs on Sundays and introduced 11pm closing, gave new opportunities to law-breakers. Hannah McConvill or Murphy was fined £7 for keeping a shebeen in Dog's Close, Great Hamilton Street. Closes in the oldest parts of town were soon honeycombed with shebeens. Many shebeeners served customers near-lethal hooch, made on the premises. Police and excise men raided a house in Anderston and discovered two illicit stills.

Mary Roseman or Skeoch was arrested for abducting a well-dressed little boy from then fashionable Monteith Row and taking him to a lodging house in Calton. A 'gentleman' was 'decoyed' into a Gallowgate brothel and robbed of his gold watch, coat, boots and umbrella. Clydeside shipyard joiners struck over a reduction in wages from £1 6s a week to £1 4s. A young servant-girl, newly engaged by a family in the Kingston district, at a monthly wage of ten bob, was summarily dismissed late one evening 'without being in possession of a farthing, or knowing a friend to whom she could apply for a night's lodging'. At an 'anti-slavery soirée', in the Astronomical Observatory, Garnethill, an American guest lecturer, Mr Parker Pillbury, gave 'a long and interesting account of the anti-slavery cause in America'.

1857   Free From Vice

The Western Bank, Glasgow's premier financial institution, failed. Shareholders, who had unlimited liability, lost the whole of their capital. City firms went bust and sacked employees en masse. In the City Hall, a grand concert was held in aid of 'unemployed sewing girls'. There were fears that the girls' desperate plight would force them into prostitution. Madeleine Smith, daughter of a prosperous Glasgow architect, was tried for the murder of her lover Pierre Emil L'Angelier, a poor clerk from the Channel Islands. The verdict of the jury was 'Not Proven'. Citizens got up a subscription for Pierre's mother and sisters. Madeleine and her lover were displayed in effigy in Ewing's Waxworks, Trongate. At a meeting in the Merchants' Hall, an appeal was launched for the 'Indian Mutiny Relief Fund'. In the wake of the Mutiny, recruiting in Glasgow was reported to be 'proceeding vigorously'.

An 'active single man' was sought for a servant's post at a house on Garngad Hill. Wages '£18 a year, with board and washing'. Mr Hunter, Miller Street, offered for sale a bay mare 'free from vice'. Clipper ships sailed from Glasgow Harbour to Valparaiso, Singapore, and Melbourne. At a soirée in the presence of the great and good in the City Hall, African explorer Dr David Livingston received the Freedom of Glasgow. Grouse sandwiches were among the delicacies to be had at William Lang's self-service restaurant, 73 Queen Street. John McLean, apprenticed to bottle makers at Port Dundas, was sentenced to 30 days' imprisonment for absenting himself from work. Robert Montgomery, keeper of the Independent Workman's Club, Maxwell Street, was fined £50 for selling liquor without a licence. The court heard that such 'sham clubs' were established solely to evade the Forbes Mackenzie Act, which prohibited tavern keepers from selling drink after 11.00pm on weekdays and all day on Sundays. Wet nurses 'whose child is not suckled or whose baby is dead' were sought by the City Medical Wet Nurse Register, King Street ('Those of temperate habits and respectability only need apply'). Gilmore Hill Hydropathic establishment promised 'the recovery of health by the power of natural agencies alone, including water in its varied forms'. Patients were accommodated 'in a fine mansion surrounded by 50 acres of beautiful parks'. Terms, 30s to 40s per week.

At the Central Police Court, 'child stripper' Janet Stupart was sent to prison for 60 days for removing wearing apparel from a three-year-old girl. At the Southern Police Court, the same sentence was passed on Jane Erskine, found guilty of selling liquor in a shebeen in Muirhead Street. WM Hill, George Street, advertised 'the American floating ball washing machine'. Prices £3, £6 and £10. Sunday schools in the East End held a Glasgow Fair musical festival in Samuel Higgenbotham's 'beautiful and extensive policies at Castle Milk'. Music, French, and Dancing were the 'accomplishments' taught at the Misses Crowther's Establishment for Young Ladies, Elmbank Street. A young woman called Jane Dickson, keeper of 'a disreputable house' in Jamaica Street, expired from an overdose of laudanum. Members of the public were invited to view the 'beautiful garden cemetery' at Sighthill, where burial plots were available from £1 to £5. A discharged Crimean veteran sought a situation 'where he would not require to walk much, having been severely wounded'.

1859   Senseless Gawkies

Police and excise officers seized an illicit still from Thomas Scott, keeper of the Working Men's Refreshment Rooms, Gallowgate. A female thief was slung into a cell at Calton cop shop and promptly went into labour – giving a new twist to the term 'confinement'. Six hundred and three Glaswegians were done for shebeening.

Amid angry protests, Glasgow Town Council proposed to let coal-mining rights on Glasgow Green. Councillors saw no problem with ensuing subsidence. As the green sank, it could be filled with rubbish. William McCulloch, Calton, unemployed for 16 weeks, died from starvation. Magistrates banned 'penny geggies' from Jail Square, at the start of Glasgow Fair. Civic leaders abhorred such 'blood and thunder dramas'. Remaining shows included 'The Tallest Woman in the World', along with 'The Caledonian Twin Sisters' – 'two heads, four ears, four eyes, two mouths and one body'. 'The Fat Lady' was eight feet in circumference. An accomplice of clairvoyant 'Spae Kristy' nicked a bag belonging to a customer up from the country for a consultation. *The Glasgow Advertiser* opined: 'We are informed that this haunt is daily frequented by crowds of senseless gawkies, who have to stand their turn while the old hag rattles off in a corner.' The body of a new-born child was found in a dung heap in Commerce Street, Tradeston.

A little girl, Catherine Gallacher, was had up for begging, accompanied by her brother, who was blind. The central police court proposed to send her to a reformatory. The fiscal asked which reformatory her mother would prefer. 'If you take this ane, sir, you may take all three; for the ither ane's blind and anither ane is just a baby.' The fiscal continued to demand an answer. 'She's going on nine years, sir. What am I to do with my other two weans? I cannot go out to work myself and this is the only one that's any use to me.' The fiscal replied: 'It's all your own fault.' Mother and child were removed – crying.

1862 Brass Crinolines

George Wilson, Argyle Street, sold 'crinolines for all classes', including 'brass mounted crinolines' and 'the patent gutta percha crinoline ... can bear a good squeeze without getting out of order'.

On New Year's Day, 'Soirées Fantastiques' took place in the City Hall, under the auspices of the Abstainers' Union. Inmates of Barnhill Poorhouse received their 'annual treat' – a special Ne'erday meal of soup, plum pudding and pies.

Fines of one and two guineas were imposed on four 'swells' – 'out for a lark', during which they taunted working men and assaulted them with walking sticks. Another four jolly japers – also 'out for a lark' – set their Newfoundland dog on three young lads walking along Dundas Street. Fines of £2 were imposed. Janet McKinlay (20) tried to kill herself by jumping into the Clyde. Rescued, she told police that her fiancé, a clerk, had 'seduced and then abandoned her'. John Lynch, World's End, Finnieston, was fined £12 10s for keeping an illegal spirit still in his house. E & S Scott, Jamaica Street, offered 'low priced clogs' at 4s a pair.

Destitute boys rioted in the House of Refuge, Duke Street. The 'arabs' broke into a storeroom, 'seized mops, scrubbing brushes, and other articles ... and demolished every pane of glass within their reach'. Police arrested 11 ringleaders. West End residents were plagued by door-to-door beggars, whose 'very appearance indicates that they are not among the deserving poor'.

Mr Charles Hengler's 'Grand Cirque Varieté' opened in a rotunda on Glasgow Green. It featured 'grand and magnificent equestrian manoeuvres, historical scenes, and brilliant spectacles'. 'Mr McArthur' opened a lavishly decorated ice cream parlour in Saltmarket. It was an immediate success, filled with 'ragged boys and half clad women – who sipped ices as if they were ladies and gentlemen of the highest position, enjoying themselves in a high-class establishment in Buchanan Street or Sauchiehall Street'.

When the City Poor House gave a soirée and ball for insane inmates, 'ladies and gentlemen took advantage of the invitation given them to witness the interesting proceedings'. In a 'daring garrotte robbery', in Langside, a youth was held by the throat while thieves escaped with £10.

Helen Campbell, a prostitute, was found dead 'in a sitting position, leaning against a wall', in Oswald Street. Death was attributed to drink and exposure. 'A great meeting of West End ladies' drummed up support for the Glasgow Magdalene Institution. Funds were sought for a 'Home for the Rescued, where reclaimed females shall enjoy a larger probation than is usual in the Magdalene Homes'. The German Gentlemen's Singing Club gave a public concert on behalf of the Night Asylum for the Houseless.

'The vigour of life' was 'restored in four weeks' by Dr Ricord's Essence of Life, 'acknowledged by the medical press to be the greatest discovery ever made'. Eleven bob a bottle; four for £1 13s.

'Men of pushing habit and good connection' were sought as agents for booksellers Blackie & Son. Salary: 15s to 20s per week. 'Lack of employment has reduced many well-doing persons of both sexes to great straits. The unemployed have to part with their clothes and furniture to procure food. Many houses lately decently furnished are now destitute.' 'The Great Western Cooking Depot' opened its seventh branch, in Washington Street. A penny bought broth, porridge, tea or coffee.

Rose Ann McAulay or Robertson – 'a woman of easy virtue' – was attacked with a razor in a house in Briggait. Her assailant was arrested in Airdrie. 'New Turkish Baths' opened in Sauchiehall Street. One bath for 2/6d; 10 for a quid. After neighbours complained of noise, police broke up 'a ball' at the Roderick Dhu Tavern, Nelson Street. A gathering of females – described as 'demoiselles de pave' – were ejected.

1864   Hotch-Potch

The American Civil War was raging. The Misses Smith, 60 St Vincent Crescent, launched an appeal for medical supplies and comforts for the hospitals of the hard-pressed Confederacy. At a meeting of ladies in the Religious Institution, St George's Place, a committee was formed to support the Glasgow Freedman's Aid Society's efforts on behalf of freed slaves. Camlachie Foundry required as apprentices 'a few steady active young men, unconnected with unions'. Apprentice John Black, employed in the Springbank Foundry, was sentenced to 30 days' imprisonment with hard labour for breaking his indentures. At Calton Police Court, three men who had contravened the Forbes Mackenzie Act by obtaining Sunday drinks in a Duke Street inn by pretending to be 'bona fide travellers' were each fined half a guinea. 'Hotch-Potch' and 'dressed tripe' at 6d per portion were on the bill of fare in The Pope's Eye Tavern, Moodie's Court, Argyle Street. The Argyll Refectory, 259 Argyle Street, advertised 'beef steak, 4d; Allsopp or Bass, 1d per half pint; wine, 2d per glass'.

There was a vacancy for a female sewing machinist at a tailoring establishment in Carrick Street. Wages 13s per week. The Glasgow Abstainers' Society had vacancies for 'female missionaries'. Cash-strapped men could doss at Greendyke Street model lodging house, where beds, with cooking and washing facilities, were provided for 1s 6d per week. Similar provisions were made for females at a 'model' in Carrick Street, Anderston. Walter Beaton & Co advertised for a 'pushing saleswoman' to take charge of the millinery department in their Cowcaddens Street warehouse; wages £30 to £40 per annum. A female assistant was required for a city fish shop. Wages from 6s to 8s per week. Garngad House, a private institution for 'the treatment of the insane and the intemperate', announced 'a few vacancies'. A city family sought a table maid – wages £10 or £11 per annum. Glasgow Magdalene Institution advertised for a matron 'of tried Christian character, to conduct the moral and religious instruction of the inmates'. Murdoch's Boys' School, Springburn, advertised for a teacher. Wages £20 per annum and 'a free house'.

The Edinburgh and Glasgow Railway advertised Glasgow Fair excursions to the Trossachs. First-Class return fare was 12s. Pleasure steamers *Inverary Castle* and *Mary Jane* sailed from Bridge Wharf to Inverary. Return fare 2s (steerage). 'Infant lions' were among the sights in Mander's Menagerie, Glasgow Green – 'admission, 1s; working class, 6d'. 'Leading styles for crinolines in 1864' were on display in Wilson's Crinoline Arcade, 226 Argyle Street. E & S Scott, Jamaica Street, sold gentlemen's elastic-sided boots for 13s 6d a pair. A rotary hair-brushing machine powered by a turbine water engine was among the state-of-the-art facilities available at hairdressers Sturrock & Sons, Buchanan Street. Comedians, tight-rope performers, and selections from grand opera were on the bill at the Whitebait Concert Rooms, St

Enoch's Wynd. The Scotia Music Hall, Stockwell Street presented 'The Gathering of the Clans' ('upwards of one hundred vocalists, dancers, &c.'). David Gray, a boy chimney sweep, was sent to prison for eight days for stealing a pair of gold earrings from the drawer of a dressing table in a house in Bothwell Terrace, Hillhead.

1866   Stirring Boys

In 1866, UK cattle were decimated by 'Cattle Plague'. *The Glasgow Herald* reported: 'Some of our most experienced veterinary surgeons are evidently bewildered, and can see no way out of the difficulty except by a process or system of indiscriminate slaughter.' Blaming 'unnatural fattening of cattle' a correspondent wrote: 'It has often struck me that sooner or later we should pay the penalty, and feel the consequence, of outraging the laws of nature.' The disease resulted in scarcity of milk. Two 'mutinous paupers' – inmates of the City Poor House – got 30 days for 'wilful and malicious mischief'. Given watery treacle with their porridge, instead of milk, they threw their plates 'violently about the room'.

In the City Hall, a New Year supper of beef, potatoes, bread and plum pudding was provided for 'the deserving poor'. Tickets were distributed by 'the Bible women of the city'. Each pauper received a packet of tea – 'which seemed to afford them a large amount of prospective pleasure'. Dr William Harthill, Bath Street, offered to cure sciatica by 'Galvanism'. On Glasgow Fair Saturday, 40 pleasure steamers left Broomielaw – most of them full to capacity long before advertised sailing times.

A reporter visited Duke Street Bridewell and inspected 'the crank' – a heavy millstone with a handle on one side. 'One is placed with every cell where hard labour is to be performed, and fixed against the wall next to the passage, where a little dial, communicating with the machine inside, shows without fail every turn of the weary handle.'

Janet Brown, convicted of stealing from a clothes line in Tradeston, asked for mercy on account of her fatherless child. Eighteen months. Nine workmen died when a boiler exploded in Isaac Beardmore's Parkhead forge. A 'baker's shop girl' wrote to the press, highlighting long working hours. Girls worked 13 hours every weekday and 16 or 17 hours on Saturdays. The sum of £40 was raised to equip the Bath Street premises of the Glasgow Shoe Black Brigade with 12 beds for homeless boys.

'A great monster meeting of miners' was held in the City Hall. Some miners worked shifts of 12 or 14 hours. Barnhill Asylum put on a concert and ball featuring 'sentimental vocalists and negro delineators', supplied by the Scotia Music Hall. Citizens paid between 1s and 4s to hear Charles Dickens read *A Christmas Carol* in the City Hall. The American Emigrant Company, Oswald Street, sought '50 single female weavers'. Gartnavel Asylum wanted two nurses – wages £12 per annum. The householder at 4 Abbotsford Place required 'an honest general servant – remuneration £10 per annum. After much deliberation, Glasgow's master bakers gave employees a Saturday half-day. In Jamaica Street, Robert Simpson sold 'Strong Suits for Stirring Boys'. 'At the sign of the golden spectacles', Glassford Street, J Lizars offered steel-framed specs – 1/6d to 7/6d a pair.

1868 Spanish Fly

The Merchants' Hall presented 'The Great American Slave Troupe and Brass Band – Composed of Untaught African Slaves from the Plantations of America'. Employers boasted that 14 Glasgow foundries were 'cleared of unionists'. Firms advertised for 'Loam and Sand Moulders unconnected with a Union'. At 27 St Enoch Square, there were 'Large Arrivals of Sardines'. The Adelphi Distillery, Gorbals touted 'Loch Katrine Malt Whisky'. Eliza Queen – 'an old offender' – copped four months for 'stealing a semmit from a clothes line on the Glasgow Green'. In the week ending January 30, 1868, the Night Asylum for the Houseless, North Frederick Street, accommodated 360 men, 120 boys, 350 women and 80 girls. Millar's, Argyle Street, offered 'The Prize Medal Air-Cushioned Dress Hat – 17/6d'. 'A young man' donated three guineas to Glasgow Royal Infirmary – 'as an acknowledgement of regret for a piece of folly'. Lorimer & Moyes, Argyll Arcade, stocked 'Spanish Fly – 3/6d a bottle'.

A personal ad proclaimed: 'E.P.M. now admits that she was wrong regarding her husband and now regrets what has happened.' Another pleaded: 'Leap Year. A Young Lady, of quiet habits, wishes a Husband. She is left in a house alone. She will be glad to correspond with anyone suitable.' At Parkhead Catholic Reformatory for Boys, cases of absconding were 'very numerous'.

Robert Whitehead, druggist, Saltmarket, sold methylated spirit 'as and for a beverage'. Fined £100. An American sea captain was 'decoyed into an improper house' and robbed of £125. Soon after, Margaret McDonald was arrested in a Bell Street pub – 'with £19 in her stockings'. Lillie & Russell, Queen Street, offered a six-hour 'Heather Tweeds' measuring and fitting service to 'Gentlemen passing through Glasgow en route for the Highlands'. Peter McGuire, Saltmarket, was fined £3 3s for 'having fought a pitched battle with Michael Rody, in the presence of 500 Glasgow roughs'. At 226 George Street, there was wanted immediately, 'Young Woman, to take charge of two Cows'.

1870   Instantaneous Portraits

Glasgow ladies launched an appeal for bandages and other medical supplies for the relief of French and German casualties in the Franco-Prussian War. The city's amateur vocal resources – the Albany Society, Choral Union, Harmonic Society, St Cecilia Society, and German Club – combined to give concerts in aid of the wounded. George Mason & Co., Union Street, advertised magic lantern 'views of the seat of war'. There were fierce skirmishes between 'roughs' and students when the latter held a torchlight procession from the old College in High Street to the new seat of learning at Gilmorehill. 'Singing classes under Signor Cunio' were on the curriculum at the Carlton Institution for the Board and Education of Young Ladies, Dixon Avenue, Queen's Park. Wylie & Lochhead, Union Street, advertised 'The largest choice of plain and gorgeous funeral equipages, including the magnificent stud of jet-black Belgian horses'. Nurses were wanted at Belvidere, the city's fever hospital in the East End. Applicants had to be able to read and write. Wages 30s per month 'with board'.

Photographer Ovinius Davis, West Nile Street, specialised in 'instantaneous portraits of children' and offered 'cartes-de-visits' at 5s per dozen. William Love was sentenced to '20 strikes with a birch rod for having obtained several articles from shopkeepers in the city under false pretences'. Old lag James Brown copped seven years' penal servitude for mugging Bernard Duffy in a close in High Street and robbing him of sevenpence halfpenny. The same sentence was passed on Ann McClinmont, found guilty on three charges of 'child-stripping'. Eliza Jackson got twelve months' for passing dud half-crowns in city pubs. Mrs Avon, Landressy Street, Calton, advertised for 'a child to wet nurse … Milk fortnight old'. Hengler's Cirque, West Nile Street, presented the Christy Minstrels ('No vulgar absurdities, but a high-class sentimental and comic concert, by gentlemanly entertainers, with blackened faces, greeted everywhere with roars of laughter and salvoes of applause.') The 'South Carolina troupe of female minstrels' performed the can-can for an appreciative audience of city gents in Davie Brown's Royal Music Hall, Dunlop Street.

Mr Dickie, Sauchiehall Street, advertised 'patent teeth without pain ... best teeth from 5s'. Dr Harthill, Bath Street, offered to treat neuralgia, paralysis, and other medical problems by means of his galvanic apparatus, promising neither 'shock nor pain'. E & S Scott, Jamaica Street, advertised 'strong boots for the sons of the working classes'. Archibald Fraser, Queen Street, sold India Pale Ale and XXX porter at 15s per nine-gallon cask and claret, burgundy and chablis at 18s per dozen bottles. 'Babies in cradle, who sprawl and kick, and exclaim "Papa" and "Mamma"' were among the Christmas toys offered for sale by Mungo Lauder & Sons, Jamaica Street.

1872 Two-Headed Nightingale

Chunks of then rural Partick were for sale – 'Suitable for workmen's dwellings'. The chairman of Govan Parochial Board lamented: 'A number of worthless people are receiving relief. They go straight to the dram shop.' William Carruthers dropped dead in George Street. Within minutes, passers-by had taken his boots. Glasgow Working Men's Conservative Association recorded 'a considerable increase in membership'.

HT Dunn, Argyle Street, offered 'Purifying Spring Medicine – Fluid Extract of Sarsaparilla combined with Dandelion and Quinine. The Alternative Medicine'. The Trades Hall exhibited 'The Most Marvellous Two-headed Nightingale'.

Elizabeth Lamont or Mushet (45) committed suicide by launching herself from a fourth-storey window. She landed head first on a bread van. At its Glasgow AGM, the Scottish Temperance League damned 'the nectar of Bass'. There were found, in Dowanhill, 'two lambs, with tar on face'. 'Mr Wallace', Dundas Street, sought 'A Lad (respectable, about 14). Wanted to learn Dentistry'.

It was alleged that 'In a large block of buildings entering from 30 Prince's Street few except noted criminals have for years past taken up their abode'. Govan Parochial Board announced that its Inspector of the Poor had been embezzling for years. Currie & Co, Jamaica Street, offered 'Waterbeds – Patent Vulcanized India Rubber'. Denholm Sabbath School raised 18s for the Glasgow Orphan and Destitute Children's Emigration Home.

1875 Vaticanism

There was advertised 'a great public meeting' in the City Hall to protest against 'Vaticanism'. The 'moneyed classes' were invited to 'come forward with prompt and generous assistance' when around 1000 workpeople, mostly women, were thrown idle after fire destroyed two cotton spinning mills in Bridgeton.

Clowns, acrobats and midgets were among the attractions in Charles Hengler's Grand Cirque, West Nile Street, which also featured 'the nondescript equestrians'. Disorderly drunk Robert Love, arrested by two policemen in Dumbarton Road, called out for assistance on his way to the lock-up. He was freed by a sympathetic crowd, who assaulted and injured the officers. Recaptured, Love was again set at liberty by the crowd. Finally secured and taken into custody, he was duly fined £3 3s with the alternative of 30 days' imprisonment. A constable was wanted for the Burgh of Govan Police. Height not less than 5 feet 10 inches; rates of pay up to 27s 6d per week. Parish churches throughout the city held a 'day of intercession on behalf of missions to the heathen'. An appeal was launched for cast-off clothing and bedding for East Park Cottage Home for Infirm Children, Maryhill. Parents were summoned before Govan Parish School Board for failure to enrol their children for elementary education under the Education (Scotland) Act. Private institutions for the education of middle-class boys and girls included Hampton Court Academy, St George's Road, Glasgow Ladies' College, Bath Street, and Blythswood Academy for Young Ladies, Blythswood Square.

City pharmacists stocked 'Cockle's Antibilious Pills', 'Cracroft's Areca-Nut Toothpaste', 'Mrs Johnson's Soothing Syrup', 'Lockyer's Sulphur Hair Restorer', and 'Widow Welch's Pills for Female Complaints'. In the Barony Poorhouse, Barnhill, two nurses were responsible for upwards of 150 hospital patients and and 300 inmates in the infirm ward. Mrs Marshall of George Street ('milk four weeks old') sought employment as a wet nurse. A governess ('fond of children') whose attainments included 'music, Parisian French, &c.,' advertised for a post, care of McKinley's Bookshop, Sauchiehall Street. A 'young lady' offered to teach 'English, rudiments of French, music, drawing' to children under 12 – 'Neighbourhood of Shettleston or East End preferred'. At Govan Police Court, Mary O'Neill, described as a 'female Fagin', was sentenced to 14 days for the crime of reset of theft. It was alleged that she induced young girl servants to steal from their employers. Catherine McCallum copped seven years' penal servitude for filching a silver watch from a man in a Gallowgate pub. The same sentence was handed out to Margaret Campbell, who pinched a watch from a drunk man in a lane near Bell Street.

The Scotia Music Hall, Stockwell Street, presented 'Sidney and Alphonse the marvellous child velocipedists' and 'La Petite Robina the wonderful child actress'. The directors of the Night Asylum for the Houseless intimated that their soup kitchen would function during the festive season. Philanthropic citizens were urged to purchase and distribute meal tickets to worthy recipients. At a 'conversazione' in the Queen's Rooms, members of the Scottish Temperance League applauded the Town Council's decision to exclude pubs from new streets formed in connection with the City Improvement Act.

1877 Dissipated Charwoman

Glasgow Museums took charge of a giraffe's tail, a green turtle (young), 24 Ashanti bronze castings and 24 skulls. 'Old Glenlivet' was 18s per gallon. Mary McGuire was jailed for 11 days, after creating a disturbance in a house in Bedford Street. 'Mary is a regular torment to her neighbours'.

Shopkeepers were in trouble, as employers locked out most of Clydeside's shipwrights. The Gaiety Theatre offered 'One of the Greatest Low Comedians on the British Stage'. William Caldwell, Gallowgate, was convicted of offering for sale 'Coloured Imperials', containing chromate of lead.

'Known rogue and vagabond' Alex McCambridge was arrested in Rutherglen Road – with a live duck under his coat. Mary Quinn or Galloway – 'a dissipated charwoman' was sent by her employer, with £1, to buy 'liquor for them both'. Mary failed to return. 'It was evident she had both purchased and consumed the liquor.'

There were complaints that communities then on the edges of Glasgow – such as the Burgh of Pollokshields – were 'No Man's Lands', enjoying city facilities without paying city taxes. William Thomson, a sweep, served 60 days for stealing a dozen eggs. George McKay was fined 7/6d for being drunk and incapable. After serving as best man at a wedding, he 'slept in St Vincent Street, in a full dress suit'.

Glasgow Orangemen were unhappy about allowing women on parades. 'The females were decidedly the most demonstrative in their behaviour, affording amusement to not a few.' At Pitt Street baths, a Mr Crichton demonstrated 'eating and drinking underwater'. Mr Andrew Bowman, photographer, Jamaica Street, offered 'Specialitie Rembrandtesque Bust Cartes'.

1881 Crutch and Toothpick

A main door flat in Hillhead went for £40 a year. Wm Younger's India Pale Ale – 'Mild, Excellent Tonic' – was available 'in cask or bottle' at licensed grocers. Thomas Duncan (16) and Alan Reid (17) broke into various cellars in Govanhill – and stole hens illegally kept by residents. Glasgow Town Council banned 'immoral literature' from Glasgow Green. Bench-seats were removed from Bridgeton Cross. Such facilities 'allowed bad characters to congregate'.

Jane Tierney (23), living with her parents at 16 Tarbet Street, jumped from a window and fell three storeys into Deanside Lane. She was drunk and her parents had refused permission for her to go out. Seriously shaken and bruised, she had no broken bones. English inventor Joseph Swan demonstrated 'his electric light' to members of Glasgow Philosophical Society, at their Bath Street rooms. The Royalty Theatre put on 'Mr Alfred Hemming's Crutch and Toothpick Family'.

The Scottish American Land Company offered cheap farms in Iowa. The American Land and Colonisation Company of Scotland touted emigration to Minnesota. One Glaswegian not tempted to leave the dear green place was American Land director Henry Cowan, who doubled up as chairman of the Partick, Hillhead and Maryhill Glasgow Company. Hengler's Grand Cirque, West Nile Street, had 'Toro – The Wonderful Performing Bull'. The Charity Organisation Society published names of citizens who were 'unworthy of public donations'. Letters to the press castigated private railway companies. Highland Railway trains wouldn't wait for Caledonian Railway trains – and vice versa. Other correspondents attacked vivisection. The city's Watching and Lighting Committee refused to experiment with electric lighting of selected thoroughfares. Twelve quarts of manzanilla sherry cost 26s. George de Fontenoy, alias the Viscount George de Fontenoy, alias Henry Edmond de Orval de Fontenoy – arrested in Rotterdam and the first Glaswegian to be deported from Continental Europe under then new extradition agreements – appeared in court charged with having stolen diamonds in Glasgow, in 1877.

1886   Rubber Balls

Angry citizens attacked 'philanthropist' and hardline Protestant fanatic William Quarrier, founder of Quarrier's Homes, Bridge of Weir. 'He deliberately proselytises Catholic children and sends them off to Canada in batches of 100.' The 'lands of Dowanhill' were for sale 'suitable for erection of tenements, self-contained houses, and villas', The Scotia Music Hall offered 'Mesmeric Manifestations'. Anti-socialists called for boycotts of the burgeoning co-operative movement. 'It will destroy the great middle class of this country.'

Kilmacolm Hydropathic Hotel promised 'Brine Baths – six times more saline than sea water'. Wallows were administered by 'experienced Bath Attendants'. Daniel McDonald, Samuel Wilson and Laurence Morrison copped five years in a reformatory for stealing three rubber balls in Queen Street. 'Negro preacher' David Nero appeared at Glasgow Sheriff Court, charged with fraudulently obtaining

£55. He was then conveyed to the dock in Kilmarnock – charged with nicking £30 'from a gentleman in Largs'.

St Mungo Homing Pigeon Society flew 'old birds' from County Monaghan to Glasgow – a distance of 160 miles. Members of a Catholic society, on a summer cruise 'doon the watter', were bombarded with stones as their vessel passed Partick. 'The perpetrators of this dastardly outrage numbered over 20, and evidently premeditated this cowardly action, as they had heaps of stones in readiness to carry out their brutal work.' There was much debate about the prospect of driving a tunnel between Scotland and Ireland. 'It would eclipse the most generous attempt at Home Rule.' Shipping lines ran direct services between Glasgow and Penang, Singapore, Manila and Yokohama.

The Victoria Hall, West Regent Street, mounted 'The Instant Disappearance of a Lady in Full Sight of the Audience'. At The Repository, Hope Street, Messrs Hutcheson & Dixon put on sale 'three Australian emus'. The eight-foot birds had endured 'a very eventful voyage'. They were twice nearly lost overboard – 'only saved through their own exertions, taking refuge in the maintop'. 'They are perfectly docile, and would make a handsome and unique addition to any gentleman's ground.'

1889 Masonic Festival

The population of Glasgow reached 550,000. A flat in West Princes Street cost £16 a year. A large family house in fashionable Buckingham Terrace was reduced to £2000. Retailers offered 'Royle's Self-Pouring Teapot – As Supplied to Her Royal Highness the Princess of Wales'. Under the running headline 'The Habits of the Cod', citizens debated whether or not cods' eggs floated or sank. There were warnings that the Lanarkshire coalfield faced exhaustion within 50 years.

The Theatre Royal put on 'A Grand Masonic Festival' – a farewell benefit for 'Mr H Lloyd, Comedian'. He took his final curtain call 'Under the Distinguished Patronage of Colonel Sir Archibald C. Campbell, Grand-Master Mason of Scotland and the Masters and Brethren of Seventeen Glasgow Lodges'. 'Tamar Indien Grillon' – 2/6d a box – was claimed to cure everything from piles to pimples. At the City Halls, 'Mademoiselle Marie Greville' – demonstrated 'The Mysterious Science of Psychcognotism'. The City Home for Boys, James Morrison Street, advertised for staff. 'None need apply except those desirous of personal work for Christ'.

Sits vac included a post of 'Good Closetmaker (fireclay)'. Messrs J & R Tennent introduced a 'Lager Beer of Surpassing Excellence'. Lonely hearts whinged in *The Matrimonial Herald and Fashionable Marriage Gazette*. Saracen Colliery, Possilpark, was for sale. Kelvinside Ladies' College, Athole Gardens, promised 'German constantly spoken in house'. The International Company of Mexico sought 'Intending Settlers' from Glasgow.

Writers of letters to editors worried about 'man-eating sharks' in the Clyde. 'It is certainly in everyone's interests to prevent these monsters getting acclimatised in British waters.' It was suggested that Clyde steamers should tow 'fully baited shark hooks'.

1892   Justice, Not Charity

Glasgow was in the grip of a trade recession. In severe winter weather, hundreds of homeless people sought shelter in the cells of police stations. Most were turned away. At a large gathering of unemployed on Glasgow Green, a committee was appointed to represent the city's unemployed, many of whom were said to be on the verge of starvation. Thousands of men, women and children were provided with food by the Gospel Army at their headquarters, the former Globe Theatre in Tobago Street, Calton. After 'General' Samuel Evans, the Army's superintendent, severed his connection with the Unemployed Relief Committee because of its alleged socialist leanings and denounced Keir Hardie and other socialists as 'dangerous revolutionaries', a well-wisher showed his approval by donating a parcel of tea and a packet of Semolina. Evans persuaded a number of jobless men to enlist in the army and navy. Soup kitchens operated in Gallowgate and St Rollox. To alleviate unemployment, Glasgow Corporation started public works in Springburn Park and Ruchill Park. The men were put to work levelling hills and breaking stones. Their wages were 1s a day on weekdays and 2s on Saturdays. They were also provided with breakfast of tea and bread and dinner of soup and bread. In Govan, at that time an independent burgh, men engaged on similar schemes got 2s 4d per day. Married men were given priority on the make-work schemes. Applicants were interviewed by the Charity Organisation Society and were asked what chapel, church or mission they attended.

At a demonstration of unemployed, held in George Square, Bailie Samuel Chisholm, who attributed all the ills of society to 'the drink traffic', was branded a 'canting, humbugging, hypocritical liar'. The demonstrators carried makeshift banners inscribed 'We demand justice, not charity'. At a meeting of the unemployed in the hall of the Glasgow Branch of the Irish National League in Gallowgate, a speaker declared that 'A man who sold his soul for 1s a day to the Corporation was false to his manhood, and deserved all the degradation that could be laid upon him'.

The Anchor Line offered steerage passages from Glasgow to New York for £4 4s. FJ Smith's 'Wild Geranium Cigarettes' were offered for sale at 107 Argyle Street. While attempting to arrest a man for theft at the North British Railway depot in College Street, Constable James Robertson of the Central Division was so badly injured that he was only able to resume duty after 119 days' sick leave. 'Original American coloured Kentucky Minstrels' performed in the City Hall, Albion Street. 'Mephisto the wonderful human serpent' was a big attraction at the down-market People's Palace of Amusements in Watson Street, off Gallowgate. At Govan Police Court, Michael Flaney got 30 days for knocking down an Orangeman and stealing his sash.

On Boxing Day, a dinner of steak pie and plum pudding was served to several thousand poor people in the City Hall. Tickets for the dinner were distributed by 'missionaries, bible-women, and the representatives of the evangelical agencies'. A 'Zulu charge' was among the attractions at a military tournament in the East End. The Glasgow Tramway Company introduced the last word in public transport – a horse-drawn tram with pneumatic tyres.

1894   Fairy Lamps

Policemen, arresting a drunk in Garngad Road, were surrounded by an angry crowd and pelted with bottles, stones and bricks. The constables were felled by the hail of missiles, while their prisoner was knocked unconscious. Maggie Irvine was sent to prison for 21 days, having been found guilty of abandoning her baby boy. On being discharged from Rottenrow maternity hospital, the young unmarried woman left the baby in a close in nearby John Street. Found alive, it was taken in charge by the parochial authorities.

At the Grand National Carnival, Cathkin Park, Miss Mary Brown, attired in a loose blouse and voluminous bloomers, made parachute descents from a hot-air balloon, landing in the vicinity of Camphill. At Queen's Park Police Court, John McKinnon and George Freeman were found guilty of stealing 'fairy lamps' from the Cathkin Park Carnival. The men were admonished. The pleasure steamer *Lord of the Isles* sailed daily from the city's Bridge Wharf. Return fare to Rothesay was 2s 6d. Summer entertainment in the city's parks was provided by the Blind Asylum Band, Glasgow Postal Band, Springburn Rechabites Band, Clyde Sub-Marine Miners' Band, and Govan Police Pipers and Dancers.

John Taylor, an assistant chemist, was fined £5 for selling laudanum to an eight-year-old boy. A girl ('smart, respectable, tall') was wanted for housework in Dennistoun. Wages 10s per month. Boxing, fencing, and Indian clubs were taught 'privately and thoroughly' by J Payne of Adelphi Street, Gorbals. Among the infectious diseases treated at Belvidere Hospital were cases of typhus, puerperal fever, scarlet fever, diptheria, and smallpox. A strong girl was required to assist in the kitchen of a house in Pollokshields. Wages 12s monthly. Restaurateur James Baillie, Main Street, Gorbals, was fined 2s 6d for 'overworking' a 17-year-old female employee. The girl had worked for over 79 hours without time off. The Royal Princess's Theatre presented the melodrama 'East Lynne'. The Grand Colosseum Warehouse, Jamaica Street, offered special bargains in 'gentlemen's straw hats' and 'boys' sailor hats'. At Glasgow Sheriff Court, sleepless tenants residing in Plantation, near the new Cessnock Dock, sought redress for disturbances caused by the marine engineering works of shipowners James and Alexander Allen. The pursuers were granted a court interdict preventing the dependents from using their steam hammer between the hours of 8pm and 6am.

The city's sanitary inspector condemned the practice of 'house-farming' in the Central district of Glasgow. Slum landlords rented whole blocks of tenements and sub-let them as furnished rooms, charging weekly rents ranging from 1s 6d to 12s. Investigators found from two to four couples sleeping in the same apartment. At the High Court, a young woman called Annie Graham was found guilty of theft by housebreaking and sentenced to three years' penal servitude. She'd stolen 6d and several articles of clothing. At Glasgow Sheriff Court, Cuthbert Keen, tailor, claimed £500 damages after being forceably removed from Portugal Street model lodging-house, belonging to the Glasgow Improvement Trust. After hearing evidence that Keen had been fighting drunk when he was ejected, the Sheriff dismissed the case.

1897   Cycling Knickers

Glasgow was enmeshed in 'the cycling craze'. City-built bikes included the 'Macgregor', 'Clyde', 'Howe', and 'St Vincent'. The Theatre Royal presented a musical comedy called 'The Bicycle Girl'. GR Husband, Renfield Street, sold men's 'cycling knickers' at 15/6d and 18/6d a pair. Pettigrew & Stephens, Sauchiehall Street, offered 'pretty coloured crepons ... specially adapted to lady devotees of the wheel'.

A New Year supper of roast beef, potatoes and plum pudding was served to 1800 elderly 'deserving poor', assembled in the City Hall. 'Not a few before beginning the meal supplied, wept visibly.' Inmates of the City Parish Poorhouse were treated to a New Year concert given by the Onward Temperance Choir. During the week ending January 22, 1897, 1298 people were admitted to Glasgow Night Asylum – 780 men, 66 boys, 351 women, and 101 girls. 'Eleven-year-old incorrigible James Montgomery' went to a reformatory for five years, for stealing two bob and treating his pals to coffee and cookies.

Messrs Brown, Barker and Bell, Union Street, sold furniture by 'easy payments' – a £9 15s oak dining room suite for 3/6d a week. 'A tidy, reliable woman', living in the Women's Industrial Home, Watson Street, offered washing and cleaning at 3d an hour or 2/6d a day. William McInally – 'Watery Willie' – was fined £5 or 30 days for shebeening in a house in Goosedubs. R W Forsyth offered 'Boys' Velveteen Sailor Suits' at the sale price of 13/9d. Russian anarchist Prince Peter Kropotkin lectured on socialism at the Queen's Rooms. James Ramsay MacDonald was selected as Labour candidate for Bridgeton.

No fewer than 93,000 Glasgow children participated in the 'Children's Fete' to mark Queen Victoria's Diamond Jubilee. 'Crouch's Wonderland', Argyle Street, exhibited 'A Living Baby, 12 inches long, 24 ounces weight, age 16 months'. James Mackay (9) stole 1s from a shop till, and was given seven strokes of a birch rod. John Forbes – 'a Slum Christian Worker' offered his services 'in any Mission Hall'.

'The Skating Palace', Sauchiehall Street, featured 'the most superb ice surface in Europe', along with 'music, electric light, warmth, and comfort'. Messrs Greenlees and Sons sold 'Easiphit Horse-Skin Boots'. The 'Louvre Fancy Goods Emporium', Sauchiehall Street, offered 'fancy Parisian clocks' and 'handsome coal vases'.

On Fair Saturday, 15 passenger steamers left Broomielaw for the Clyde Coast. A return fare to Rothesay on RMS *Columba* or *Iona* cost 2/6d. A dozen bottles of 'Royal Lochnagar Balmoral Whisky' cost £2 2s. 'Roderick Dhu Old Highland Whisky' was recommended 'by analysts and physicians'. 'Dr Haines' Golden Specific' was claimed to 'positively cure the liquor habit'. Ads trumpeted: 'It Never Fails'. 'Dr Williams' Pink Pills for Pale People' were peddled for 'asthma, paralysis, consumption, scrofula, and St Vitus' Dance'. At the Britannia Music Hall, Trongate, attractions included young Harry Lauder, and 'Dr' Walford Bodie – 'ventriloquist, scientist, hypnotist, and electrician'. 'The Achmed Ibrahim Troupe of Arabs' appeared at the Scotia Music Hall. The Royal Princess's Theatre presented 'Go-Won-Go Mohawk – The Famous and only Indian Actress', in a melodrama called 'Wep-Ton-No-Mah – The Indian Mail Carrier'.

1899   'Vesta Vendors'

A policeman, patrolling his beat in the vicinity of Glasgow Cross, found a dead shark, measuring over eight feet long. It was placed in a barrow and taken to the Central Police Office. Cathcart School Board advertised for a female certificated assistant for Queen's Park Public School. Salary £60 per annum, rising by annual increments to £100. At Glasgow Sheriff Court, James O'Brian was sentenced to 60 days' imprisonment with hard labour for deserting his wife and child 'whereby they became chargeable to the Parish of Glasgow'.

Joe Wesley, 'favourite burlesque Negro comedian' and Master George Macfarlane 'the Boy Marvel' sought professional engagements. At the Central Police Court, John Kavanagh was fined £7 for 'Sunday whisky hawking'. Donations were sought to promote the work of the Glasgow Poor Children's Fresh-Air Fortnight scheme which sent slum children to the seaside, and for the Weary Workers' Rest, which offered vacations to 'female Christian workers who are unable to take a holiday out of their limited means'.

In the Glasgow Justice of the Peace Court, the SSPCC obtained a warrant for the removal of William Ferrier (9) to the Slatefield Industrial School in Gallowgate. The boy sold matches 'at very unseasonable hours' in Argyle Street and slept in doss houses. A warrant was also granted for the removal of another child 'vesta vendor', Mary Nisbet (11), to the Maryhill Industrial School. Like Ferrier, the child sold matches in Argyle Street. Fining city employers for dangerous breaches of Factory Act legislation, Sheriff Boyd warned them that 'it was his intention to take no excuse on the grounds of ignorance of the law'.

Over 100,000 children took part in Glasgow Children's Day, held in the city's parks. The sole refreshment provided by the city fathers was tap water. With the outbreak of the Boer War, army reservists in Glasgow Police Force were instructed to rejoin their old regiments for service in the Transvaal. The Chief Constable informed the men that they would be re-instated in the force when they returned home. Glasgow Parish Council gave the first of a series of winter entertainments, consisting of 'cinematograph views' and gramophone selections, for their pauper charges in the City Poorhouse. The inmates of Hawkhead Asylum, Crookston, were entertained by the Titwood Amateur Minstrels. The occupant of a small flat in Queen Margaret Drive advertised for a 'girl for general housework' – wages,

25s per month. The body of a newly-born baby was found floating in Princes Dock. On examination, it was discovered that the child had been stillborn.

1900   Yarra-Yarra Brand

Messrs Deane & Co, West Nile Street, did a line in 'Portable Turkish Baths' – 15 bob a time. Michele Valente, owner of an ice cream parlour in Parkhead, was done for shebeening. The population of Govan reached 76,000. An unemployed miner hanged himself from a tree in Polmadie. A steamer called the *Titanic* plied between the Clyde and the Caribbean.

Messrs C B McNeill & Sons, Craighall Bottle Works, Bishop Street, Port Dundas, advertised 'Masonic Bottles A Speciality'. The firm touted its wares in *The Glasgow Examiner* – which proclaimed itself 'the Irish and Catholic Organ for Scotland'. The Boer War was in full tilt. Messrs Lizars offered 'Cinematograph showings of the Transvaal War'. Govan's Lyceum Theatre put on 'Soldiers of the Queen'. The Grand Panorama, Sauchiehall Street, mounted 'The Battle of Waterloo'. Margaret Winn, 7 University Gardens, appealed to 'every Margaret in Scotland' to send 1s to endow a bed at the Scottish War Hospital. Glasgow Corporation Tramways Department refused to have advertising inside its trams. Robert Cran – 'an elderly man' – was accused of bigamy. For Mr Cran, second time around was indeed a triumph of hope over experience. The second Mrs Cran 'lost her heart to a coloured man lately come to the house'. Messrs Campbell Blair, Howard Street, offered 'Australian Burgundy – The Albatross Brand, along with the Yarra-Yarra Brand'. Glasgow schools were open on Christmas Day. The city's Watching and Lighting Committee examined samples of straw hats suggested as summer wear for police officers. There were 7000 telephones in the Glasgow area. 'Frau Lager' advertised her finishing school in Koblenz.

1903   Electro Vigour

In 1903, a family house in up-market Hamilton Park Terrace cost £1100. Rents in fashionable Dudley Drive were around £21 a year. Civic leaders held a service to commemorate the 1300th anniversary of the death of St Mungo. Peebles Hydropathic Hotel offered Glaswegians 'A German Bath in Scotland'.

There were 12,000 telephone subscribers in Glasgow. An exclusive telephone line cost £5 a year. At the City Halls, concert-goers applauded 'The Celebrated and Popular Dennistoun Amateur Minstrels in Their Plantation Melodies'. Sits vac included an opportunity for 'A House-Table Maid (Catholic)'. On the Forth and

Clyde Canal, the *Fairy Queen* and *May Queen* left daily for Kirkintilloch, from Port Dundas. Return fare 1s. Evening excursions 9d.

The Glasgow Herald offered readers free maps of the Balkans. Glasgow Corporation City Improvements Department advertised for 'Musical Associations or Public-Spirited Individuals' to give renditions in model lodging houses. The Mission to the Outdoor Blind for Glasgow and The West of Scotland appealed for cast-off clothing. Under-cover investigators from the Pharmaceutical Society of Great Britain found numerous Glasgow grocers and chemists using unqualified staff to purvey chloroform and laudanum. In November 1900, 12 such transgressors were done. 'There is no place where there are more glaring or persistent offences than in Glasgow.'

The Royalty Theatre put on 'Are You A Mason?' – preceded by 'Hushed Up'. The Gramophone and Typewriter Co, 12 City Road, published 'A Special Scotch catalogue', featuring Harry Lauder and the Kiltie's Band. Dr A. McLaughlin, 25 Buchanan Street, promised 'Weak People Made Strong – With Electro Vigour.'

1907   Baby Farmers

There was an outbreak of bubonic plague in Gorbals. Suspected cases were removed to Belvidere Hospital. A previous outbreak of plague in Glasgow, in 1900, had claimed 16 lives. It was reported that, in Cowcaddens and other slum districts of Glasgow, 60 per cent of babies were born without the help of doctors or midwives. 'One result was that not only did the child often die, but nearly every second mother taken into hospital died of puerperal fever.' In the Bute Hall, Glasgow University, there was a 'free fight among the students' during the Graduation ceremony. The event was described as 'one of the worst ever experienced in the University annals of Glasgow'.

An official of the SNPCC reported that cruelty to children was on the increase in Glasgow. 'In the case of 23 parents, the condition of the children was so shockingly bad that prosecutions had to be ordered, and in every case a conviction was obtained, 13 parents being sent to prison, four admonished, while six had sentence delayed by the Sheriff.' By 32 votes to 5, Glasgow Corporation defeated proposals for music in city parks on Sundays and for the opening on Sundays of childrens' playgrounds.

At Glasgow Sheriff Court, two 'baby farmers', Christina Deans and Marion

Nicholson, were convicted under the 1897 Infant Life Protection Act and sentenced to six months' imprisonment. The women had taken charge of infants in return for cash premiums. Deans and Nicholson then 'farmed' the children out to women in the Springburn area, promising to pay them 2s 6d a week. The Court heard that the accused used blackmail to obtain additional payments from the childrens' natural parents. When police searched their house, they found a box containing 12 birth certificates relating to children belonging to people in Edinburgh.

The staff at Girgenti, Glasgow Corporation's Ayrshire retreat for 'pauper inebriates', reported that attempts to cure the inmates by means of drugs had met with failure. Girgenti housed 130 habitual drunkards of both sexes. Inmates of Barnhill Poorhouse complained that 'Life in Barnhill is becoming almost unbearable', after staff turned the Poorhouse recreation ground into a croquet lawn for their own use. Kelvinbridge Registry, 429 Great Western Road, offered 'splendid openings for all classes of domestic servants'. The junction of Renfrew Street and West Nile Street was described as 'the favourite spot in Glasgow for loafing and dangerous hooligans'.

1911   Nurse Rae

A West Regent Street money-lender rejoiced in the name of 'Adam Smith'. A paddle-steamer jaunt to Rothesay cost 1s. 'Dinner and plain tea' ran to an extra three bob. 'Nurse Rae' offered massages at 237 North Street. At St Rollox police court, a young man called Brimo Buchan copped 14 days, for slinging an inkstand at the governor of Barnhill Poorhouse. The Scottish Finance Company, Union Street, asked: 'The Rent Is Due – What About The Cash?' There was founded the Glasgow branch of the Anti-Socialist Union of Great Britain. In Hillhead, the Motor Brougham and Car Co Ltd offered 'The Smokeless and Noiseless Napier'.

At 405 Sauchiehall Street, 'Professor Kalogy – The Great American' offered 'expert clairvoyance'. At 322 West Princes Street, 'Madame Stella' promised 'Crystal Vision'. 'Queer-rolling' flourished then as now. James McLardy, described as a 'Green prowler', haunted Glasgow Green and Cathedral Square 'for the purpose of preying on drunk men'. The Coliseum Theatre featured 'Lipinski's Forty Dog Comedians'. In Broomielaw Ward, 73 out of every 100 houses made human life 'indecent and painful'.

The Rudge-Whitworth Depot, West Nile Street stocked 'The First and Only Motor Bicycle to Beat 60 Miles in the Hour'. Cranston's Tea Rooms, 28 Buchanan Street, offered 'The American Soda Fountain – Dispensed by a Lady Expert'. Fraudsters set up fake emigration offices, took deposits on 'fares' – and vanished. Licenced grocers and publicans watered their whiskies. A crowd of 700 watched an illegal bare-knuckle fight in Gorbals. Dr D G McLennan – 'with his London Lady Assistant' – offered 'Lessons in Glasgow to Ladies and Gentlemen attending their Majesties' Court (full procedure)'. The Scottish Exhibition, Kelvingrove Park, advertised 'Arctic Camp and Equatorial Colony' – along with a 'Joy House'. The Pavilion Theatre put on 'Sydney James's Strolling Players'.

1912   Orphans For Export

E H Bostock's Scottish Zoo in New City Road featured Miss Violet Maud Rogers, 'Glasgow's pluckiest vocalist', who promised to 'sing a favourite Scottish ballad in a cage of lions'. Dr George Bell Todd, a well-known Glasgow GP, appeared in court charged with performing an abortion on a Gourock women, who subsequently died. The city's sanitary authorities reacted swiftly to a threatened epidemic of typhus fever in Commercial Road, Gorbals. Over 50 people were removed to the city's reception house for suspected fever cases.

The Duchess of Argyll opened the new 40-bed Glasgow Cancer Hospital in Garnethill. Artistes engaged by the Corporation's Court and Alleys Concerts Committee, dedicated to performing in the slums of Glasgow, gave their opening concert of the season in a backcourt in Green Street, Calton. The congregation of Paisley Road Baptist Church, Plantation, mourned the Reverend John Harper, who had gone down with RMS *Titanic*. At a meeting held in the Merchants' House, Lord Provost Stevenson suggested that the city should stop educating orphans and young offenders in local institutions and export them instead to the Colonies. The Australian Government had set the ball rolling by offering £6 per head and a free elementary education for child emigrants.

At Glasgow Sheriff Court, Suffragette Annie Rhoda Walker or Greig, 'a young lady dressed in black', was sentenced to seven days' imprisonment for breaking a window in a motor car belonging to a local bigwig, Sir Thomas Mason. Emily Hickson or Green (47), a Suffragette described as 'tall and stylishly dressed', broke five plate glass windows in the Wellington Street frontage of Messrs Copland & Lye's exclusive shopping emporium. Engineering apprentices stormed Suffragette premises in Sauchiehall Street. A Suffragette spokeswoman said 'There was a strong sporting instinct among women, and they were quite prepared to take as well as give any blows that were going.'

At Glasgow Sheriff Court, James Scott (50) was sent to prison for 60 days for falsely claiming to have been knocked down by a tram while crossing Saltmarket. Michael Higgens went to Borstal for two years for assaulting mourners near Janefield Cemetery by knocking off their tall silk hats and kicking them along the street. The first of several new 13.5 inch guns for the Royal Navy was dispatched from William Beardmore's Parkhead Forge. The Metropole presented a melodrama called 'From Mill Girl To Millionaire'.

1913 Protestant Cooks

Ads advised: 'Doctors Orders! On No Account Omit Golden Shred Marmalade From Breakfast.' The Empire Theatre featured 'Katie Sandovinia, The Lady Hercules'. The Botanic Hall, Queen Street, promised 'All Diseases Cured with Herbs'. The body of a baby was found in a tin box in a Partick flat. An incoming tenant opened the box 'because a very disagreeable smell pervaded the room' – which had been previously occupied by a 22-year-old woman.

Charles Ward (15) – 'boarded out as an outdoor patient of Glasgow Parish Council' – shot himself on a farm near Forfar. 'The Lodge, Carnoustie. Estd 1900' was forthright about its services – 'Alcoholism'. The 'De Groot Fostgate Treatment' – for the same complaint – could be had at 153 St Vincent Street. Ruthelina Sands or Fowler admitted allowing her children to live in a brothel at 30 Canal Street, Port Dundas. Police found her 'helplessly drunk with her head in the fireplace'. 'She took in immoral women and a number of men.' Six bottles of Talisker cost 24s. Glenlivet was 21s a dozen.

The Glasgow Herald opened an office at 17 Boulevard de la Madeleine, Paris. The Savoy Theatre exhibited 'The Real Argentine Tango'. The Royal Polytechnic, Argyle Street, purveyed 'Meat Teas for Theatre Parties in the Restaurant Louis XVI'. Newspapers ran pages of ads for intending emigrants. 'Reap the Benefit of Canada's Prosperity. Canada guarantees work on the land for every willing worker and employment at good wages for all domestic servants.' At home, bigots sought the services of 'Protestant Cooks and Maids'.

On Christmas Eve, the Savoy Theatre featured 'The Four Krays'. Charles Douglas was charged with 'an unnatural offence', in a Govan stable.

Part II
1914–1945

1914   Masonic Socks

Thirty city Orangemen, armed with rifles, guarded the colours of the Ulster Volunteers as they marched through Glasgow. Glaswegians were introduced to Macfarlane Lang's 'Orange Cream' biscuits.

A South Side newsagent was charged with retailing indecent postcards 'depicting people in the latest American fashion – X-Ray skirts'. A defence witness claimed: 'Transparent skirts are yet to be seen in Glasgow – but the fashion is on the way.'

Charged with failing to maintain his wife, an Anderston man claimed he had in fact plenty of money – he ran a brothel in Springburn Road. After tenants of a Partick flat emigrated, the landlord found in the basement equipment used to produce counterfeit half crowns. Ads for a Buchanan Street emporium urged women to buy 'Convent-Made Lingerie'.

During Fair Week 1914, 70,000 Glaswegians descended on Rothesay. Between 15 July and 22 July, city police arrested 460 drunk and incapable Glaswegians, along with 550 who were drunk and disorderly. Rutherglen's chief sanitary inspector stated: 'Over-indulgence in alcohol by both male and female members of the community forms a serious barrier to public health reform.' As the First World War loomed, army deserters appeared from every part of Glasgow. One man had been AWOL since 1896. As war was declared, city newsboys charged a penny for ha'penny newspapers – provoking a storm of anger from West End citizens. Newsboys shouted: 'War and football – all the results!' City freemasons and their wives were urged to knit socks for soldiers.

Walking sticks and tobacco pipes, lost property from city trams, were given to wounded soldiers at Stobhill Hospital. Other items left on the 'caurs' included rosaries, corsets, boxing gloves and alarm clocks. A militant Suffragette horse-whipped a member of His Majesty's Prison Commission for Scotland, outside Duke Street jail where Helen Crawford was on hunger strike. Crawford had been jailed for breaking windows at an army recruiting office in Gallowgate. On release, she was 'in a state of collapse'. 'A respectably dressed young woman' left a suitcase with the attendant in the ladies' lavatory at Custom House Quay. The suitcase contained a dead baby. A rag-picker found another dead infant in a bin in a Shawlands backcourt. Glasgow's Night Shelter for the Houseless admitted 991 men, 368 women, 57 girls and 34 boys.

1915   Vermin-Proof Shirts

Glasgow grocers advertised 'Tea and Cocoa Tablets for Our Boys in the Trenches'. Glasgow soldier James Quin accidentally discharged his rifle while sitting in a tram in Sauchiehall Street – and killed squaddie Simon Lawson, a wounded man repatriated from a German POW camp. The Metropole Theatre, Stockwell Street, featured 'Up Boys and At 'Em'. The Glasgow Empire offered 'Shell Out – The Wonderful Revue'. Copland and Lye, Sauchiehall Street, advertised 'The New Vermin-Proof Shirt – A Preventative from the Infection of the Trenches – 6d each'. R & G Lawrie, Renfield Street, offered bagpipes 'For Recruiting, Marching, Or Inspiring Our Brave Soldiers On To Victory'.

Glasgow Corporation Tramways enrolled 700 female conductresses and issued them with green straw hats and long Black Watch tartan skirts. Scotstoun's experiment with women posties was declared 'highly successful'. By June 15, there were more than 12,000 Belgian refugees in Scotland. A Belgian horse-flesh butcher opened in Gallowgate. The Grand Central – 'Glasgow's Latest Restaurant De Luxe' – featured 'The Belgian Ladies Band from the Liege Conservatoire'.

At Scotland's first tribunal under the Munitions of War Act, 31 Glasgow coppersmiths were fined for going on strike. Boys at Battlefield School manual instruction class received a Government order for 200 trench periscopes. Lost property held by City of Glasgow Police included a pony, a horse, and a black-faced ewe.

Two youths were admonished after breaking Glasgow harbour by-laws by swimming across the Clyde. The magistrate remarked: 'The feat was characteristic of British pluck.' In response to possible raids by 'terrorising Zeppelins', half Glasgow's street lighting was extinguished from midnight. The Defence of the Realm Act restricted alcohol sales. Shebeeners filled the gap. Edith Foster or Kelly was fined £10 for shebeening in Lyon Street, off Garscube Road.

Glaswegians were urged to 'See the Ambulance Train in Central Station'. Private Harry May, Glasgow's first Great War VC, arrived home to a hero's welcome. City pubs sold Carlsberg lager – 'Not German, Nor Even Brewed by Germans.'

The Toyland at Trérons, Sauchiehall Street promised 'Everything for the Nursery' – including war games ('The Rage of the Season'), model trenches and barbed wire entanglements, motor ambulances, soldier dolls in khaki, and 'Hand Grenade Banks for Boys'.

1916   Shell Belles

Boys at Glasgow schools were taught 'interesting and practical woodwork' – making crutches for wounded soldiers. Frank Connolly (15) was convicted under the Defence of the Realm Act, having 'misused an electric torchlight by flashing it in College Street at night'. Six members of the Cowboy gang were each fined 10/6d after entering a Dennistoun pub and threatening customers with a toy gun. Two members of the Redskins gang, who'd caused a disturbance in a city dance hall received 10 days in jail. Govan shebeener Sarah Gillan or Docherty copped a £30 fine for selling a man a half bottle of home-made whisky.

Placards on Glasgow trams read: 'To shave the boys at the Front, hand your old razors to the conductresses.' A soldier's wife was sentenced to three months' imprisonment for child neglect. A court heard she spent her army allowance on methylated spirits. For distributing a socialist leaflet, Kenneth Stewart received a month's imprisonment, with hard labour. Ignoring a conscientious objector's plea for exemption on religious grounds, a sheriff opined: 'Is this not nonsense? You are in the world, and must take your part in its duties like other people.' Glasgow artist Harry Bathgate, another conscientious objector, was fined £2 for failing to enlist under the Military Service Act. Glasgow Licensing Court refused to allow publicans to employ barmaids in lieu of barmen eligible for military service.

In August 1916, as the Somme offensive raged, Glasgow cinemas showed 'The Battle of the Somme – The Official Record of the Great Advance – Undoubtedly the Most Wonderful Film Ever Produced'. As casualty lists mounted, costumiers Darling & James, Sauchiehall Street, offered 'A Large Selection of Ready-to-Wear Mourning Garments'. The Glasgow Society for Women's Suffrage organised 'Cheer Up! Clubs', with cooking and dancing classes for soldiers' wives. Glasgow soldier Walter Haddow, serving with the Royal Naval Division, was killed in the early stages of the Battle of the Somme. He was 17 years old.

At the McLellan Galleries, an 'Active Service Exhibition' featured 'Real Trenches and Dug-Outs As At the Front', along with 'Trench Concerts – Given by Men Just Home from the Front'. The Alhambra Theatre featured 'The Lena Ashwell Firing-

Line Concert Party – Direct from the Firing-Line'. The Coliseum Music Hall mounted 'A Day in a Dug-Out – The Topical Show with a Humorous Touch'.

A Glasgow munitions tribunal heard that women war workers – 'the shell belles' – could afford grand pianos. One girl stated her wages were £3 1/4d a week. As Christmas approached, the Royal Polytechnic department store, Argyle Street, advertised 'Vermin-Proof Underwear – A Great Boon to our Brave Men'.

1917 Tommies' Lonely Lassies

With food supplies menaced by U-boats, Glaswegians were told: 'Eat Less Bread – Save the Wheat and Help the Fleet!' At the Woodlands Institute, the Women's Legion opened Glasgow's first communal kitchen. The manager of Glasgow Corporation Tramways appealed for walking sticks for wounded soldiers. Passengers were urged to hand over their sticks to conductresses.

Bridgeton's Olympia Music Hall presented 'Tommies' Lonely Lassies'. As the Battle of Passchendaele raged in Flanders, the big attraction at Green's Whitevale Carnival was 'A Tour of the Ypres Trenches – Private George Wilson VC Will Conduct You Past the Bullet-Swept Corners'. The Alhambra Theatre – 'The Resort of the Elite' – featured 'High Explosives – A Brilliant Musical Laughlette'. At Pollokshields School, teachers and pupils presented former pupil Sergeant Major John Skinner VC with a gold watch and an ivory and gold mounted Malacca cane. Skinner had been wounded seven times.

'Motresses and conductresses' from Possil Tramway Depot entertained wounded soldiers at Maryhill Depot Hall. Items left on trams included 530 purses, 315 pairs of gloves, 37 rings, 19 rosaries – and an officer's collapsible bed. A Govan man, described as a 'bogus VC', was arrested on suspicion of theft. Peter Bradley, Port Dundas, was fined for 'keeping premises for cock-fighting' – the first conviction of its kind in Scotland. Samuel Levy (11) received six strokes of the birch for assaulting a girl with a knife.

Hundreds of Glasgow Fair holiday makers slept on Portobello Beach, because boarding houses were full. Holidaymakers lucky enough to secure accommodation slept on the 'hot bed' system. Apparently undeterred by her 1916 conviction, Sara Gillon or Docherty was again charged with selling whisky – 'so bad it was undrinkable'. Female bookie Mary Ventry was arrested with 45 betting slips and £7 in cash in her possession.

In Ibrox, where an 'abnormal number of young women work long hours on munitions', infant mortality was 130 per 1000. The downfall of James Kelter (11) was attributed to 'the lure of the ice cream shop coupled with the attraction of the picture house'. Convicted of pinching a wallet containing five 10s notes, he was sent to the training ship *Mars* for five years. There was an 'epidemic' of pocket-picking in the St Rollox area of Glasgow. Elizabeth Campbell (13) was fatally wounded in a rifle range accident at a showground in Moncur Street, Calton.

1918   Socialist Brass

Glaswegians were told: 'The Coal You Go Without Is Taking the Americans to the Front.' Conscientious objector George Moodie (19) was fined £2 and handed over to the military. He claimed he'd acted according to teaching received at a Socialist Sunday School. Glasgow police banned the city's Socialist Brass Band from playing in the streets. On his release from Peterhead prison, Glasgow revolutionary John MacLean was greeted by thousands of supporters at Buchanan Street station. Glasgow Trades and Labour Council rejected left wingers' demands to establish a Glasgow Soviet.

The Coliseum Music Hall put on 'Singing Wounded Tommy'. A Glasgow soldier on leave wrote: 'I went out with the original expeditionary force in 1914, and for three years and six months we have been in the firing line. There are very few of us left, but what there are could surely be brought back for home service.' The Metropole offered 'Home From the Trenches – A Great Moral Lesson Play'. Munitions factory worker Maggie Regan, Gorbals, was fined £5 or 30 days for possessing two matches at work. One of the matches was concealed in her hair. Queen Street, Govan, was described as 'the home of shebeens'. In one week alone, three shebeening cases were heard at Govan Police Court.

William MacGregor (13) stole food from a Byres Road shop. He was sent to the training ship *Empress* for three years. Mary Mullins, described as a destitute Irish girl, was jailed for two months for abandoning her baby in St Andrew's Cathedral. Glasgow cleaner Margaret Moon, a widow, got 30 days for stealing sheets and bed mats from Barnhill Poorhouse. Margaret White, described as the 'well-dressed wife of a munitions worker' – was fined £5 or 30 days for the theft of two gold rings from a city jeweller. As Glasgow endured a massive outbreak of Spanish flu, the Royal Polytechnic offered 'Pure Wool Flannel Belts – A Grand Preventative Against Influenza'.

A Scottish Training School for women police officers opened in Newton Place, Charing Cross. The Scottish HQ of the Women's Royal Air Force was established at the Adelphi Hotel, Argyle Street. John O'Halloran, a member of the Calton Redskins gang, was jailed for 30 days after assaulting the owner of an ice cream saloon with a leather thong – known to the Redskins as a 'coish'. An 'educated West End girl (30)' advertised for 'a patriotic man – a gentleman by birth and education'.

1919   League of Mistresses

A car containing a wedding party was ascending Hill Street, Garnethill, when its brakes failed. The vehicle ran backwards, gathering speed. The driver reverse-turned into Cambridge Street – and went rear first through the window of an up-market millinery shop. A 'War Memorial Hall', capable of seating 8,000 people, was proposed for George Square. During a visit to Glasgow, Native Americans conferred a sub-chieftainship of the Iroquois nation on Glasgow Corporation's halls manager. His Iroquois name was Sogoweehay – 'Chief Generous the Giver'.

On 31 January 1919 – 'Bloody Friday' – while police battled left-wing demonstrators in George Square, hundreds of other Glaswegians rampaged along Argyle Street, smashing shop windows, and looting clothes, shoes and soft furnishings. At a meeting to protest against persecution of Jews in Eastern Europe, Private Jack White, Glasgow's Jewish Great War VC, received 'a massive ovation'. An 18-year-old youth stole a parcel from Central Station. It contained 39 ladies' corsets. The Kearney High-Speed Railway Company offered to build an electric passenger railway through Glasgow's harbour tunnel linking Finnieston and Tradeston. A train would leave every minute, taking 25 seconds to cross the bed of the Clyde.

In response to the demands of a domestic servants' union, wealthy Glasgow women threatened to set up a 'League of Mistresses'. One employer claimed maids should appreciate wearing black dresses and white aprons. 'It is a mark of respectability.' If that was so, opined a union activist, why didn't mistresses don such apparel? Absent-minded passengers left 4,213 umbrellas on Glasgow trams. To celebrate the Treaty of Versailles, Glasgow Corporation laid on a lavish civic luncheon. Labour councillors damned the event as extravagant and unnecessary. Thousands of protesting ex-soldiers marched to Glasgow Green. One of their banners read: 'Not a Drum Was Heard, As Off To The Luncheon They Hurried'. Another banner proclaimed: 'A General's Widow, £25,000 – Tommy's Widow, 13/9d'. On Armistice Day, 11 November, Glasgow came to a standstill. 'Most men stood to attention, while women and children also waited reverently till the 120 seconds had passed.'

In Parliament, Glasgow MP Neil Maclean quizzed the Minister of Pensions about the case of 4661 Private George Armstrong, 18th Battalion, Highland Light Infantry, wounded at the Somme, gassed in Flanders, discharged from the army minus a leg. 'He is compelled, in order to earn a living for his wife and three children, to play an organ on the streets of Glasgow.'

1920   Breakfast Rat

In late summer, Maryhill publicans shut their shops early – 'because everyone was on holiday'. Thwarted bevvy merchants took instant umbrage – and rampaged through the area smashing windows and looting pubs and shops. Sixty thousand Glaswegians marched against landlords' attempts to increase rents. Tens of thousands of workers struck for the day in sympathy. One scheming landlord tried to nobble tenants' leader and Red Clydesider Emanuel Shinwell, by maliciously lodging a case claiming he was in rent arrears on his Govan flat. The case collapsed in court when it was shown that the eviction action had been lodged without a valid notice to quit having been issued beforehand.

Another Govan tenant, pursued for rent arrears amounting to 9d, told a court he refused to pay on principle. 'I was having my breakfast when a rat came in and stole my ham. ' It was estimated that Glasgow contained 13,195 houses officially unfit for human habitation. Most were inhabited. A skint Glasgow squaddie tried to travel from Euston to Glasgow – on the carriage roof of an express train. He was undetected till Preston, where he accidentally activated the train's communication cord.

Two days after a city woman was charged with bigamy, her first husband was killed during a boxing tournament. Her 'bereavement' didn't prevent conviction. Another bigamist had been wed, in 1915, to a woman who already had 13 children. It was revealed that at the time of the second 'wedding', he was the father of an equally large family in Partick. A 10-year-old city boy was sent to a reformatory for nine years – after stealing four boxes of chocolates and a tin of condensed milk. Forty thousand teetotallers demonstrated for a 'dry' Glasgow. Opponents painted a 6ft-high slogan on a wall in Sauchiehall Street. It read: 'PROHIBITION IS THE MADNESS OF THE FEW FOR THE SUPPRESSION OF THE MANY!'

For the first time, Glasgow councillors voted to have no alcohol during their annual 'inspection' of the city's Loch Katrine water source. At Glasgow Fair, three city families headed for Saltcoats – where a landlady had booked them all into the same room. The landlady was fined £5 for fraudulently taking three simultaneous deposits. Following a flood at the Cathcart works of G & J Weir Ltd, workers caught a number of trout in the factory's smiddy. Jokers suggested one of them should be stuffed – and presented to Lord Weir as a memento.

1921   Eastern Princess

As unemployment mounted, councillors voted to set up a municipal agency where wealthy citizens could recruit maids. The council also backed moves to identify all married women in its employment whose husbands also had full-time jobs. Revolutionary leader John MacLean headed a march on the City Chambers by thousands of unemployed Glaswegians. Their banner read: 'Glasgow's Unemployed. Fighting 1914 – Starving 1919'. While unemployment in the city grew at up to 1000 people a day, Labour councillors tried angrily to halt civic plans to spend cash on honouring the Prince of Wales with the freedom of the city. Thomas McGuire (9), sent out to beg, collapsed from hunger at the door of a house in Rutherglen Road.

Hundreds of unemployed citizens dug coal from riverbank outcrops and abandoned pit bings. Giving evidence during the trial of a fortune teller nicked during the Kelvin Hall carnival, a Glasgow detective told a court that the spey wifie had informed him: 'You have travelled over water.' Had you travelled over water?' asked the defence. 'Yes, the Kelvin.'

James Fleming (21) – 'dressed as an Eastern Princess' – was arrested during a masked ball and charged with stealing eight sets of bagpipes. On 15 March, 1921, women sat on criminal juries in Glasgow for the first time. In Shettleston, an illicit distiller told police that a still found in his house was 'an Irish musical instrument'. 'A respectably dressed middle-aged man' had in his house at 74 Abercromby Street, Bridgeton, 35 revolvers, six hand grenades, a bomb, 955 rounds of revolver and rifle ammunition, detonators, 21 packets of gelignite, a coil of fuse wire, holsters, magazines – and a bayonet. Sinn Fein affiliations were suspected.

In an attempt to save Glasgow from sin, adherents of the Partick Bethel, Merkland Street, backed by a sister congregation in Govan, held all-night prayer meetings. A Strathbungo woman divorced her husband, after discovering a letter addressed to him by one of his male friends. The letter began: 'My dear girlie'. It concluded: 'Best love, yours, Willie'. On Sunday, 10th July, 1921, the temperature in Glasgow reached 107 degrees fahrenheit. Govan Parish Council agreed to change the name of Merryflats Poorhouse to 'Southern General Hospital'. A city man was convicted of the 'low, mean fraud' of obtaining subscriptions 'on the pretence that these were for the purpose of prayers being offered for the souls of dead soldiers'.

1922   Take Food

Civic dignitary Sir Samuel Chisholm said 'Young women stream into Glasgow almost every day of the year.' Volunteers met them at railway stations and steamer landings. 'The number of women who are stranded is almost incredible.' Prosecuting a woman for brothel-keeping at 67 Robertson Lane, Glasgow's procurator fiscal demanded automatic prison sentences for such offences. 'it is a means of improving the moral atmosphere of the city.'

William Robb – Glasgow's 'king of dog thieves' – went down for 30 days after stealing a guard dog from premises in Dobbie's Loan. In Govan, Labour council candidate J N Docherty was charged with supplying taxis to take electors to the polls. One of Mr Docherty's co-accused was a Mr George Galloway. One driver said: 'I gave my services free because Mr Docherty had an Irish name.' Glasgow branch of the British Legion claimed: Young Irishmen obtain council jobs to the exclusion of ex-servicemen and ratepayers.'

Thirty-one workers at Glasgow's upmarket Ca'doro Restaurant were charged with stealing bacon, ham, chickens, eggs, puddings, potatoes, beans, cakes, butter, biscuits, bananas, apples, cooked meats, sandwiches, sugar, fish – and soap. Clydeside revolutionary Harry McShane told Glasgow's 70,000 unemployed men and 14,000 unemployed women: 'If it comes to starving, to hell with law and order. It is better to break the law than to starve. If you are starving, take food.'

Drug addicts forged prescriptions. Thieves not only robbed city homes while residents were on holiday during Glasgow Fair, but actually slept in householders' beds. A Renfield Street fortune teller told an undercover cop 'You will marry a tall, dark man and live to a good old age.' A few minutes later, she gave an identical reading to another customer – who also happened to be a police officer. Police claimed prostitutes haunted Gordon Street, Hope Street, St Vincent Street and Sauchiehall Street.

Red Clydesider and councillor Emanuel Shinwell was among parents who refused to purchase school books for children when Glasgow Corporation withdrew free books from city schools.

A stair cleaner, found dead in her St Andrew's Square garret, had hoarded more than a hundredweight of pennies and ha'pennies. Magistrates established a 'Purer Language on the Street' committee – which put up posters at cinemas and football grounds, urging Glaswegians not to swear. In a house in Lochlea Road, Newlands, police found a distillation plant and a number of barrels.

Glasgow Sheriff Court heard that second-degree initiates of the Knights of St Andrew – a quasi-Masonic Roman Catholic secret society – had 'neither opinions nor consciences of their own, save as the Grand Master directs'.

1923   Free Love

More than 51,000 homeless Glaswegians applied for and received overnight accommodation in police cells. They weren't admitted until 10.30pm and were turned out at 6am – without food. Hunger marchers trudged from Glasgow to London and returned to denounce Communist Party march organisers who, they claimed, had used them as a cash-raising stunt. Marchers alleged that collections in towns en route simply vanished. They said they'd even had to sleep in mortuaries. They claimed CP leaders had failed to pay them the promised maintenance of 22/6d a week during the protest.

Police said Shettleston was Glasgow's major venue for illicit distilling. It was a 'growing industry'. 'Professor Eastburn' was charged under the Venereal Diseases Act 1917. He distributed leaflets offering to cure venereal diseases at £22 a time. His 'cure' for nervousness cost £34. One victim handed over £88. Married man John Barnes, Cramond Street, took up with a young Rutherglen woman, and induced her to purchase from a city chemist a quantity of sulphate of zinc – a poison. He put it in his wife's morning tea. It didn't work, and Barnes went inside for 18 months.

Moses Hetherington, a shopkeeper, William Strang, a shop manager, and grocer William Burton put ads in the city papers offering 'jobs for girls'. They then sexually assaulted applicants – including a 14-year-old girl. A city bigamist was done for obtaining money from women by convincing them he was 'selling teeth on the instalment plan'. Glasgow labourer John Mason admitted neglecting his four children. He had begun to court a 22-year-old female workmate. Mason expounded 'free love views' to the young woman.

A Garnethill widow put a lonely hearts ad in city papers – and was contacted by music hall artiste John McGahey. McGahey moved in with her, and convinced her he was about to gain a substantial legacy. He induced her to withdraw her investments of £800 – and took all her jewellery.

Govan Parish Council heard large numbers of children were being sent to the poorhouse because their parents were homeless. A councillor said: 'The stigma of the poorhouse should not attach to soldiers' families who cannot get houses.' While claiming buroo money, a Glasgow man tried to augment his income by hiring a barrel organ. He was grassed off by a competitor who wanted his pitch. In order to listen to newly introduced crystal set radios, Glaswegians stripped earpieces from phone boxes throughout the city.

1924 Meths and Vinegar

Police raided a West End flat said to have 'rivalled a night club in opulence'. A number of women were charged with running a brothel. Mary Kirby, Henry Ashton, and Robert Wilson Muir were jailed for dressing up as glamorous women, using the names of well-known stars of stage and screen, and luring middle-class men to a Glasgow flat. Victims were either blackmailed or attacked and robbed.

A Russian-born Glaswegian was convicted of preparing and selling methylated spirits as a beverage. In his St Andrew's Square flat, a few yards from the HQ of the City of Glasgow Police, he concocted a drink consisting of meths boiled with brown vinegar. A court heard Glaswegians consumed this potion 'in very large quantities' at 1s per gill. Unemployed ex-servicemen were taken on as 'dancing partners' in city halls and clubs. One man admitted he had been taken home – 'just once' – 'by a rather mature and stout wealthy widow'.

The mummified body of a two-year-old child was found in an ashpit in Anderston. Police suspected the child was a victim of 'baby farming'. During 1924, newspapers ran dozens of ads placed by single women who sought private adopters for their babies. Baby farmers took the children for 'adoption', charging the mothers a 'premium'. Often the children were killed and disposed of in rivers, canals and quarries. Police stated they would interview a number of city women known to arrange 'adoptions'.

Two jobless Anderston men, Hugh McAllister (17) and Owen Fitzpatrick (22) stowed away on a vessel bound from the Clyde for Boston. For five days they sweated in a hiding place behind one of the ship's boilers. They were caught and confined to a storeroom. In Boston harbour, they broke out, and headed inland. They gave themselves up on hearing that the captain might be fined for their escape – and worked their passage back to Glasgow. King's Park man Charles Thomson stowed away from Montreal to the Clyde. He'd been lured to North America by promises of high wages at Henry Ford's automobile plant. On his return, he warned that Ford's claims of high wages were nonsense. He had been so poorly paid he could scarcely cover his digs in Detroit.

1925   Johnny Ramensky

At a meeting in the Orange Halls, Baltic Street, Bridgeton, held to recruit for the recently formed British Fascisti, the Earl of Glasgow said: 'The Fascisti believe in force, but only against the Communists.' Communists and fascists clashed at the gates of Alexandra Park, where both groups held open-air meetings. Denouncing a popular East End clergyman as a 'communist', fascists disrupted a religious service in Calton. Blackshirts also trashed the Hope Street offices of *The Sunday Worker*. Three Glasgow men were charged with murdering Indian pedlar Noorh Mohammed. A large number of Indians, some of whom had travelled large distances, attended Mohammed's funeral in Riddrie cemetery.

Glasgow's depute town clerk argued that the city needed an additional 94,000 houses to alleviate overcrowding and slums. Glasgow building workers threatened to halt work on housing schemes throughout the city if the Corporation ordered C & J Weir's prefabricated steel houses – which one councillor denounced as 'glorified corn-beef tins'.

Johnny Ramensky (20) – 'one of the most expert cat burglars whom police have had to deal with for a long time' – got 18 months for house-breaking in the West End. On one night alone, he'd entered six houses. Martin Sweeney, a member of the Dirty Dozen gang, was jailed for three months for assaulting a man with a lead-filled bayonet scabbard.

Coiffeur des Dames, Paisley Road West, advertised 'Shingling and Bobbing by Experts in Our Private Rooms.' His Lordship's Larder, St Enoch Place, offered a table d'hôte dinner for 4/6d. Glasgow Newsboys' League and Home appealed for cast-off clothing. The Sons of Rechab 'Go Forward' Tent, Dennistoun, visited Easterhouse for their annual teetotal picnic. Eight young Glaswegians, stowaways on the steamer Saturnia, en route for Canada, were returned to Glasgow and fined

£5 each. They said they were unemployed and hoped to find work in Canada.

The convenor of Glasgow Corporation Tramways Department stated: 'There is no evidence that the day of the tramcar has passed.' The Rev J A C Mackellar, Cathcart, said: 'Conversion of the Jew is not the impossible thing some people imagine.' The Rev Dr Watt, of Glasgow Cathedral opined: 'Citizens are putting the maxims of Marie Stopes in the place of the Beatitudes.'

Thirty wax heads and a wooden coffin were pinched from A E Pickard's wax-works in Miller Place, Saltmarket. Two police constables, making an arrest in Glasgow's Plantation district, were severely mauled by a hostile crowd. The Gateside Laundry, Duke Street, advertised 'Bagwash 2s'.

1926   Fossilised Rolls

Food parcels given to families of locked-out Shettleston miners contained 'green-moulded black pudding, rotten eggs and cheese, and fossilised rolls'. Glasgow men were lured to 'a certain lodging house in Paisley', where they were robbed. Razor gangs were reported 'busy' in the East End of Glasgow. Lascar seamen and firemen clashed on board the steamer *City of Sparta* in a Govan graving dock.

In Bridgeton, there were outbursts of 'gang terrorism'. Fifty youths, aged from 14 years upwards, fought in a pitched battle between the Lollipops and the Kent Star Boys in Shuttle Street, near Albion Street. The Lollipops also clashed with the Romeos. In court, a leader of the Norman Conks gang admitted carrying a bayonet down the leg of his trousers. He claimed he needed the weapon because the rival Billy Boys were after him. Catherine Clark – 'a middle-aged woman' – was jailed for 18 months for performing an abortion. Arthur Hunter was fined 10s for operating a 'Glasgow Shop Lottery' at his Bridge Street shop. 'Madam Signa', palmist, Newton Street, predicted a rosy future for a client – who turned out to be an undercover policewoman sent to arrest her.

On the eve of the General Strike, which began on 4 May, 1926, dozens of pipe, brass and flute bands led a huge May Day procession to Glasgow Green. As essential services ground to a standstill, 'The Roll of Voluntary Workers' opened at St Andrew's Halls. Members of the British Fascisti were ordered to report to the group's Pitt Street HQ. Tramways supremo James Dalrymple resigned when the city's tramways committee voted to reinstate 316 employees sacked for taking part in the General Strike.

The Govan United Ministers' Council fulminated against Sunday opening of children's playgrounds. In Rumford Street, Bridgeton, the infant mortality rate was 142.9 per 1000 births, compared with the city-wide rate of 107 per 1000. Tram conductor John McNeish was ordered to pay Hughina McInnes breach of promise damages of £100. The Locarno – 'Glasgow's new Dance Salon' – opened in Sauchiehall Street with a 'Hogmanay Gala Night'. The hall's 'Thé Dansants' – 'with professional dance partners and teachers' – cost 2/6d. At Wylie Hill's, Buchanan Street, a 'Victory Pedal Car' cost £7 10s – several times a shop assistant's weekly wage. The Anchor Donaldson shipping line offered £3 fares to Canada – 'for approved families, farm and household workers'.

1927   Dalmarnock Castle

Styling himself 'Sir Leslie Martin of Dalmarnock Castle', a Glasgow man took up with a Gallowgate widow. Believing their mother was to wed a knight, her children told neighbours and reporters they were going to live in a castle. A grand wedding ceremony and reception was booked with an upmarket city centre restaurant. 'Sir Leslie' promised to collect his betrothed in his limousine, for triumphant progress to the celebrations. A large crowd, controlled by police, gathered outside her tenement. 'Sir Leslie' never showed up.

Government figures revealed 13% of Glaswegians living in single-ends – the highest proportion in the UK. At least 27% of Glaswegians lived more than three persons to a room. Veteran city cracksman William Herd (64) said to have been a regular gambler in Monte Carlo, described as resembling 'a respectable business man' – was jailed for the umpteenth time after being caught in commercial premises in Rutherglen. He was said to have enough explosives to destroy the entire building. Henry Sands was fined £1 for charging admission to a dance in his room and kitchen flat. Police found 51 young people in the house. It took police two hours to search elderly beggar Harry Livingstone, who wore five overcoats and three pairs of trousers – crammed with a stone of copper coins, 1000 fag ends, and several hundred keys.

A Glasgow tinsmith, arrested in possession of six gallons of home-distilled whisky mash, admitted he had used his working skills to manufacture a number of stills for friends and neighbours. On 11 July, 1927, serious violence erupted during Glasgow's annual Orange Walk. As the procession returned to the city from fields near Cambuslang, hundreds of young men broke into 'We are the Brigton Billy Boys' and attacked a 'Catholic' pub. As the Partick contingent returned to base, opponents waved green flags – and a pitched battle broke out at Partick Cross.

In Sauchiehall Street, hundreds of Glaswegians became extras during filming of Sir Harry Lauder in the role of city grocer Dickson McCunn in John Buchan's *Huntingtower*. A number of city boys were recruited as members of the 'Gorbals Diehards'. A Glaswegian disabled ex-Great War soldier won £3 3s and a silver bowl as Scotland's first mouth-organ champion. On Armistice Day, 1927, poppies were in such demand in Glasgow that supplies ran out early in the day. Cars were despatched to Edinburgh to bring back more poppies.

1928 Unshrinkable Combinations

Frank Matthews, 'a clever educated, cunning swindler', who passed himself off as Lord Inver, Lord Leangarth, Lord Culross of Fife, and Colonel Matthews DSO, absconded without paying his bill at a Glasgow hotel. He was jailed for 60 days with hard labour. Robert Stewart was arrested at Glasgow Cross, with gelignite detonators and fuse wire in his possession. Police raided the Carlton Club, Virginia Street, and arrested 38 men for illegal gambling. They included 'Jews, Poles and Russians'. In Joseph Brady's Bridgeton house, police found 'a complete still, properly connected up and in the process of making whisky'. Brady sold the whisky at 8s per bottle.

Rival gangs clashed in the Gaiety Theatre, Argyle Street, near Anderston Cross. Glasgow presbytery of the United Free Church of Scotland complained about congregations being distracted by the airliner 'City of Glasgow' taking citizens on Sunday joyrides from Renfrew. An ex-serviceman – 'disabled with limp, no pension' – sought work as a 'watchman, storeman, hoistman, caretaker: anything considered'. A girl who threw one of her shoes at an Orange Walk in London Road was fined £2. Moses Buchanan, Renfield Street, offered free passages to Australia, 'to girls for domestic work'.

A 16-year-old domestic servant was charged with putting turpentine in her mistress's medicine bottle. James Tait was fatally stabbed during a gang fight between the South Side Stickers and the Calton Entry. Glasgow businessmen promised 'revelations of a startling nature with regard to civic extravagance'. A Tollcross householder wanted a maid 'used to children, no Catholics'. Fining a street bookie, Bailie J Bain Fraser castigated council tenants who gambled. 'The ratepayers are rated in order to subsidise these people, and yet they spend the money on betting. I think it is deplorable.' Glasgow's Fresh Air Fortnight Fund sought donations. '30s will give a child a fortnight at the seaside.' Five thousand citizens took part in a 'Glasgow Historical Pageant' to raise cash for a new dental hospital.

A Territorial soldier fired at a crow from a moving train and killed a nursemaid walking with her fiancé on Cathkin Braes – two miles away. He was jailed for three months. An auto-giro flew over the South Side. James Campbell, Stockwell Street sold 'Irish Duck Eggs' from 1s a dozen. His ads insisted: 'No Foreign Eggs of any Description Sold.'

Tréron's advertised: 'Unshrinkable Combinations for Ladies – Price 5/11d'. The Glasgow Sun-Ray Centre, Sauchiehall Street, promised to banish gout, deafness, head noises, grey hair, baldness, and neurasthenia.

1929   Savages

Crowds watched Glasgow's new 'robot policeman' – traffic lights at the junction of Hope Street and Sauchiehall Street. Two human coppers were also on duty – 'to ensure that the automatic traffic signals would be obeyed'. Charged with breach of the peace, a Govan man claimed: 'The people who stay below me are deliberately pumping hot air into my house by a mysterious apparatus every night when I go to bed.' 'Try my bed,' he urged the magistrate – who declined the offer and put him on probation. Lord Provost Sir David Mason criticised city companies who'd failed to help Glasgow's cash-strapped Royal Infirmary, which needed 'at least £20,000 annually'.

Demanding the 'right to live' 150 unemployed men from throughout Scotland left Glasgow on a five-weeks' march to London. 'They told pathetic stories of bitter weather and forced marches through blinding snowstorms and over ice-covered roads.' Single men aged between 19 and 35 were promised: 'Free Passages and Assured Work On Canadian Farms'. At top store Pettigrew and Stephen, Sauchiehall Street, a 'Genuine Eugene Permanent Wave' cost £2 2s – more than a week's wage for many workers.

Thousands of Scots contributed to a national fund for distressed miners. Donations came from places as far apart as Jura and Brazil. Gifts in kind included two tons of potatoes and a diamond and ruby ring. General Sir Ian Hamilton told Glasgow Gordon Highlanders' Association that the Government could take 25,000 men off the dole by building a mid-Scotland ship canal. Sir Henry and Lady Mechan gave £5,000 to the Western Infirmary to purchase radium for cancer treatment.

Professor A A Bowman of Glasgow University told Glasgow Rotary Club: 'Britain's slum dwellers are in the scale of humanity lower than the Hottentot – a fine race of savages.' Slum dwellers were 'on the level of Australian bushmen'. Bowman compared them with 'the degraded natives of Alaska'. City magistrates allowed Sunday use of the new Crossmyloof skating rink to a skating club. Councillor John McSkimming disagreed. He was particularly disturbed by the fact that Sunday skating sessions were accompanied by 'the raucous strains of a jazz band'.

Dirt-track racing, featuring 'Steel-Nerved Dare-Devil Dirt Track Terrors', drew crowds to Glasgow's new White City Speedway, Ibrox. Customs officer Robert Gillespie admitted stealing 52 bottles of whisky from a Washington Street bonded warehouse. He said: 'I was under the influence of the heavy alcoholic atmosphere and the whisky I consumed during the day.'

1930   Canine Casinos

Forty baton-wielding young men formed a 'Workers Defence Force' for the Communist Party's May Day rally. Right-wing opponents set up 'The British Fascists' Special Patrols'. Scotland Yard denied it was investigating corrupt Glasgow councillors. Unemployed and hungry, Richard Harkins grabbed a black pudding from an Argyle Street chip shop, hid it in his jacket, ran off – and was fined 7/6d. The pudding was worth 3d.

A Whitecraigs resident wanted St Kilda designated a home for Glasgow alcoholics. In his report for 1929, Glasgow's chief constable revealed his force had arrested 40 bigamists and 286 meths drinkers. They had also birched 51 juveniles. Disguised as Indian pedlars, detectives arrested Annie Wilson or Missori – 'widow of a coloured man and proprietor of a café at Anderston Quay' – for harbouring immoral women and allowing men to smoke hashish.

Neds in the news included the Liberty gang and the Villagers. It was claimed they used 'back slang' – a secret language. An East End minister claimed there were 11 gangs in the vicinity of his church. He proposed to wean them off razor slashing and rioting in cinemas by taking them rambling. A Bridgeton contractor bought a horse from Tiree – and discovered it would only obey commands in Gaelic. Retailers urged Glaswegians to try 'Dago Sauce'.

Giving evidence against a street bookie, a police superintendent said: 'No sooner do you arrest one bookie, than another takes his place.' In Govan, police nabbed a female bookie – who had round her waist a satchel containing £13 and 97 betting lines. She also had a three-month-old child in her arms. Her husband was also an illegal bookie. When he was absent, his wife acted as substitute.

At Glasgow's latest cinema, The Kelvin, Argyle Street, every second seat was a 'chummy' – a double seat without a central arm-rest. Thomas Scott was jailed for selling bottles of 'S-Ray Attraction' – guaranteed to cure everything from cancer to carbuncles. The bottles contained Glasgow tap water.

1931   Dollar Watch

A Govan clairvoyant told an undercover cop: 'You have two children and are separated from your wife.' The policeman happened to be single. She told a civilian witness: 'You should sever all home ties and go abroad, since you are young and single.' The man had a wife and two children. The spey wifie's lawyer said 'Such cases are common at church bazaars.'

Another Govan woman told a court that every day for 18 years, her husband had sent their children out of the room while he thrashed her with a leather belt. 'The trouble began when I helped a neighbour with her washing.' Sentencing a Shawlands man for having an unlicensed radio set, a Glasgow sheriff described radio as 'a scientific abomination'. Faced with a case of retailing obscene pictures, the same sheriff opined: 'The morals of the community, from my experience, do not require to be corrupted.'

A runaway bull took refuge behind the counter of a Duke Street newsagent's shop. It was removed only after the counter had been sawn away. The president of Glasgow Chamber of Commerce claimed the city's reputation as 'a centre of well-developed revolutionary tendencies' obstructed attraction of new industries. In 1931, Glasgow contained 40,000 single-ends. Glasgow Council of Juvenile Organisations claimed city gangs were 'renouncing the street feud' and expelling members who came into conflict with the police.

There died at his home in Connecticut, USA, Briggait-born watchmaker Archibald Ballantyne, inventor of America's first 'dollar watch' which became the stable product of the Ingersoll Watch Company. Newspapers reported on a 'fluctuating population of Indian seamen' accommodated at Queen's Dock. As they prepared for Ramadan, they were described as 'the only Mohammedan community in Glasgow'.

The Scottish Society for the Protection of Wild Birds revealed that a duck had nested 17ft up a tree in Dawsholm Park – where it reared five ducklings. Canada deported ex-pat Glasgow families deemed 'liable to become charges on public funds'. One family had three children – all of them born in Canada. A woman charged with stealing chocolate from a Glasgow shop said in court she had done it to 'get evidence with which to divorce my husband'. Fearing for her sanity, the court ordered her medically examined. A few days later, it was explained that the women was of Russian origin, and what she had really meant was 'I want to give my husband a reason to divorce me.'

1932   Buroo Schools

A court heard that on the South Side of Glasgow, citizens consumed an 'obnoxious drink' composed of methylated spirits boiled with wine and vegetables. The mixture was drained off and fermented. In court on January 1, Mary Lauder boasted of having consumed 20 gills of red wine and five pints of beer. 'Happy New Year, your honour,' said Mary, as she left the dock.

With 125,819 people unemployed in Glasgow, desperate city women were forced to become maids in upmarket areas. At 6 Queen's Gardens, the Ministry of Labour opened a training school for maids. Two men charged with stealing 11 cars said they'd been taught to drive at one of Glasgow's 'buroo schools'. The Medical Research Council claimed Glasgow's overcrowding was a consequence of working class people 'having a fondness for herding together'. Unemployed citizens disrupted services at Glasgow Cathedral, demanding that ministers condemn the Means Test.

An unemployed woman abandoned her month-old daughter on a South Side doorstep. A note with the baby read: 'I cannot find a situation. This is the only way to save my baby. I will come back for her in six months.' It was revealed that, during 1931, free meals to councillors cost £4345. Councillors also had rental use of a number of Trossachs mansions owned by Glasgow's water department.

Resident in a 'model' since coming out of jail in 1923, George Dickson got three years' penal servitude for possessing a mould designed to produce counterfeit sixpences. A court heard Dickson was known in the city as 'The Coiner'. Chief Constable Percy Sillitoe warned of the dangers of cocktail-drinking among young Glaswegians. He urged members of the teetotal Band of Hope to pay home visits to known cocktail-drinkers. The president of Glasgow University's all-women Queen Margaret Union said female students did not drink cocktails. 'I would never allow it.'

Glasgow Rover Scouts resisted demands from Scouting's London HQ to wear khaki hats instead of Balmoral bonnets. Thanks to anti-pollution measures, it was claimed that herring had come up the Clyde as far as Yoker. Glasgow Corporation reluctantly agreed to allow housing scheme newsagents to open on Sundays. A cache of drugs, including cocaine, was found in a wood at Anniesland. James McElrick threw one of his boots through a window of a police station. He explained: 'My pal is in Barlinnie and I want to be with him.'

1933   Govan Tweeds

Lord Provost Swan promised: 'Glasgow's homes of the future will be palaces of delight.' Chief Constable Percy Sillitoe attempted to give a lecture on big-game hunting in Africa, to an audience of unemployed citizens in a Partick Cinema. The audience heckled him and sang 'The Internationale'. Glasgow branch of the Red Cross appealed for £5000 to provide clothes for unemployed people.

A boy who had no parents, no home, and lived rough on the streets, sleeping among rubbish and old newspapers, was sent to an approved school. Glasgow Sheriff Court heard the case of a man who hadn't maintained his family since 1919. A party of 52 young men – 'drawn from the ranks of the unemployed' – left Glasgow for Argyll, where Government had set up an 'afforestation camp'. Govan's Pearce Institute installed two handlooms to teach unemployed citizens how to weave tweeds.

At a beauty parlour for dogs in Anniesland, business was reported as 'booming'. The Brinkley Studio, Rose Street, invited debutantes to be photographed 'before or after' their presentation at Court. The Anchor Line offered cruises from Glasgow to Madeira and the Canary Islands. Giffnock Junior Imperialists put on a play at the Lyric Theatre. Wylie and Lochead urged Christmas shoppers: 'Choose Your Gifts in the Colourful Atmosphere of Our Eastern Bazaar.'

Glasgow magistrates 'declared war' on meths drinking – 'which has increased steadily since the war'. Sentencing three boys to six strokes each of the birch, a sheriff opined: 'Juvenile crime is becoming intolerable in Glasgow.' Two 'well-dressed married women' were jailed for performing an abortion on a girl of 18. Thieves concealed themselves in the Picture House, Possilpark, and left in the wee small hours with the safe. When the safe was blasted open at the Astoria Cinema, Possil Road, the explosion was heard 'throughout the district'. A police source claimed: 'Unemployed quarrymen, accustomed to explosives, are behind the spate of safe-blowing in Glasgow.'

Labour councillor Jean Roberts wanted unemployed people enrolled in a 'municipal brigade', to clean tenement stairs twice weekly. As jobless Glaswegians sought weekend relief by hiking in mountains and glens, a temperance campaigner attacked the new outdoor movement. 'A common sight in the countryside is a party of irresponsible youths, complete with plus fours down to their ankles and shrieking stockings, carrying a banjo, a football, a ricketty, and a tea urn, making themselves a nuisance to everyone'.

1934   Free Pies

Edward Hilley, Bonnar Street, Bridgeton, admitted fiddling his gas meter. He said: 'I needed the gas for the still, which was for making whisky.' At the Pavilion Theatre hundreds of unemployed Glaswegians attended a free matinée of 'Red Riding Hood'. During the show, comedian Harry Gordon distributed free pies – donated by a city restaurant. Six hours after an East End woman gave birth to her eighth child in a Bridgeton tenement, her husband died from a penetrated lung, caused by a piece of shrapnel lodged in his body since the Great War.

Gang warfare raged in Depression-battered Glasgow. Innocent bystander James Dalziel (35) was stabbed to death when rival gangs clashed in the Bedford dance hall, Gorbals. One member of the Billy Boys went down for four years with hard labour – after razor-wielding Billy Boys attacked Celtic fans at Bridgeton station. During a gang fight in Cowcaddens, terrified pedestrians sheltered in closes and shops. When police tried to break up a gang battle in Garngad Road, they were met with a volley of stones. Three members of the Derry Boys were jailed for smashing windows at Sacred Heart School, Bridgeton.

In Carntyne, a worried householder complained there was a stray sheep in his garden. Officers from Eastern Division arrived in a Black Maria and took the vagrant into custody. Harry Keir – 'The People's Painter' – had his first exhibition. By trade, he was a house painter and sign-writer. Communists attacked a fascist meeting in Renfield Street. The battered blackshirts took refuge in an office block – and had to be rescued by a police patrol wagon. A Partick resident found a peacock strolling in his garden. 'A constable shoved the bird under his arm, mounted his cycle, and conducted his passenger to the station.'

A mystery explosion, made by an improvised bomb, damaged the army recruiting office in Bath Lane. In Dalmarnock, ranked as Glasgow's worst-hit industrial area, 23.4% of citizens were in receipt of public assistance relief. The Clydesdale Supply Company, Sauchiehall Street, demonstrated television pictures transmitted from the Baird Television Company's studio at Crystal Palace, London. A Glasgow paper opined: 'Television is not far from being as popular as radio.' Elizabeth Hillhouse (59) was fined 5s at Maryhill Police Court for 'begging for alms'. It was revealed she lived in a six-roomed West End flat and had two working sons. Spec builders promised: 'A home of your own in Clarkston will give you an all-the-year holiday'.

1935 Nudists and Nomads

The Salvation Army claimed young Glaswegians were in moral danger from dance halls. 'They are a more serious menace than drinking or gambling.' The Sally Ann proposed to visit halls and escort young women home late at night. Among the 500,000 Glaswegians who left the city during Glasgow Fair 1935 were a growing number of nudists. Mosspark tenants complained to the Corporation about a 'nudist camp' on the banks of the Cart. Other sun-worshippers were reported camping in the hills above Drumchapel.

'Nomads' – groups of young men and women out of work and denied benefit under the hated Means Test – lived rough in woods and glens in the countryside near Glasgow. A nomad camp could contain 100 people. One nomad said: 'In tramps' jargon, we are "belly-thieves". We steal to eat.' Glasgow had 100,000 unemployed in 1935, equivalent to the population of Aberdeenshire. Young members of the National Unemployed Workers' Movement organised a cyclists' 'hunger run' from Glasgow to London. It was revealed that some clerks employed by the Clyde Navigation Trust earned less that 30s a week.

The uncompromising novel *No Mean City* was published in October 1935. Councillors were outraged. The book was denounced as a 'gross libel on Glasgow'. Letters in the press welcomed *No Mean City* as telling it like it was. 'Children are sick and suffering. The husband spends the last sixpence on the horses. The horse loses, the wife scolds, and the man breaks up the little bit of furniture.' During November 1935 alone, the RSSPCC prosecuted 21 Glasgow parents for cruelty and neglect of children. All 21 were convicted.

In Anderston, a mob of more than 1000 people attempted to rescue a man who'd been arrested by two police officers. Twenty men and boys were arrested during a police raid on the 'long close' – an infamous illegal gambling venue in Cowcaddens. At 250 Paisley Road West, police raided a 'disorderly house frequented by naval officers'. Weapons used in violent clashes during the 1935 Orange Walk included hammers, bottles, razors, iron bars, pokers, rolling pins and knives.

1936 Purity Drive

Police in Govan took custody of a red, white and blue canoe – found moored to a tree on Pollok Estate. 'Ultra-Modern Houses' – all at less than £400 – went on show at the Housing and Health Exhibition at Kelvin Hall. A workman engaged in preparing the site of Glasgow Corporation's new infectious diseases hospital at

Cowglen 'suddenly disappeared into mine galleries believed to be at least 150 years old'. He was uninjured. At Cathkin Park, a 'purity drive' to stamp out swearing by football fans resulted in a supporter being fined £2. Television was demonstrated at the Scottish Radio Exhibition at St Andrew's Halls. Glaswegians were told it would be at least five years before 'practical television' came to Scotland.

Looking out of his window in Townmill Street, off Alexandra Parade, John Wallace saw a roe deer vanish up a close in Whitehill Street. Mr Wallace secured the animal. Police told him: 'You'll be allowed to keep it if no owner comes forward.' A Queen Street trader advertised 'Huge and Well Selected Stocks of Maids' Uniforms at Popular Prices'. Twenty-five trace horse boys, employed in the streets of Glasgow, took part in the city's annual trace horse parade.

In the East End gang warfare intensified. Police reinforcements, including mounted units, were drafted in. Police officers were attacked and injured by bottles and stones. Guilty gangs included the Derry Boys, the Norman Conks and the Savoy Arcadians. City magistrates vowed to impose tough sentences on gang members – and alleged that gangsters' fines were often met by frightened shopkeepers paying protection money.

Unemployed Glaswegians protested against new Unemployed Assistance Board dole scales. Lord Provost John Stewart claimed almost 40,000 citizens faced reduced dole. 'Individual reductions will range from 1/6d per week to 7s per week. The total loss to unemployed householders in Glasgow will be approximately £230,000 per year. A man and wife on relief of 26s per week in Glasgow would have it reduced to 24s per week.'

Bridgeton's Independent Labour Party MP Jimmy Maxton attacked the Means Test. 'It is well within the capacity of this country, without running it into bankruptcy or financial difficulties, to pay unemployment scales at the rate of £1 per week for each male or female, 10s a week for a wife, and 5s a week for each dependent child.' 'Milk bars for children' opened in Anderston, Bridgeton, Gorbals and Govan. A third of a pint cost a ha'penny.

1937   Aggie The Bookie

A man was jailed for 30 days for defrauding Glasgow Corporation transport department of 10d. At Parkhead Forge, 1500 engineers struck for a penny an hour increase. At an exhibition in the McLellan Galleries, citizens learned how to construct 'refuge rooms' to protect against poison gas in the event of air raids on

Glasgow. Despite official claims of 'returning prosperity', the city had more than 86,000 unemployed people. George Armour (24), who'd walked 100 miles from Glasgow in search of work, collapsed from exhaustion at the Falls of Cruachan, Argyll. He hadn't eaten for 14 hours.

Police raided houses in Springburn and Possilpark and seized components of an illegal still, along with hundreds of bottles and several gallons of illicit spirits. Agnes Miller Mitchell – 'Aggie the Bookie' – was charged with offering a ten-bob bribe to a police officer in a close in Scotia Street, St George's Cross. She was alleged to have said: 'Here ye are. Now keep away.' In a copyright dispute over who had the right to publish and perform the 'Ould Orange Flute', the tune was whistled, sung and played on a mouth-organ in Glasgow Sheriff Court.

Six unemployed men – 'pests who invade George Square at night for the purpose of interfering with down and outs' – were fined £1 each. In Blochairn Iron and Steel Works, Garngad, a workman killed a female otter, which might have come from the Molendinar Burn or the Monklands Canal.

At Carmyle Miners' Welfare Institute, William Ward (19) consumed 19 pies in a pie-eating contest. He then said: 'I'm away home for my supper.' More than 200 men were arrested during a police swoop on an illegal gambling club in Olympia Street, Bridgeton. Two clerks at Parkhead buroo were done for forging banknotes. Police raided premises in Bath Street and Buchanan Street, alleged to be 'secret libraries' lending and retailing pornography. Membership was said to cost £1 a year, with books borrowed at 5s a time.

The Band of Hope warned Glaswegians: 'The cocktail habit is slowly enmeshing the young womanhood of the country. To the less stable mind its social appeal is not the least of its dangerous attractions.' Finnieston woman Elizabeth Brockett became ill in a tramcar in London Road. She gave birth to a daughter as the tram passed Bridgeton Cross. Newspapers highlighted widespread consumption of 'boot polish cocktail', which consisted of a bottle of lemonade mixed with meths, metal polish and boot polish.

1938 Granny Blackburn

Hotel proprietors and householders complained about reports that a 'sun-bathing and naturist' club was to open in the St George's Cross area. 'We have been annoyed for a fortnight by callers, asking for information about the club,' said a hotel manageress. 'Those seeking information have all been men, most of them apparently well-to-do people.' A 13-year-old schoolgirl pick-pocket was described in court as 'a menace in the streets and particularly in crowded warehouses'.

'Granny Blackburn' – a.k.a Mary Reilly – who'd sold newspapers at the corner of Stockwell Street and Argyle Street for many years, was found dead in her Gallowgate flat. She left £4000. Glasgow Corporation allowed Scottish hunger marchers to sleep in municipal halls. In court, a pick-pocket extolled the attractions of the Empire Exhibition in Bellahouston Park. 'Who would attempt to pick-pockets in the East End when all roads in the West End lead to the Exhibition and provide such experienced men as ourselves with golden opportunities for pocket-picking?'

Amid much emotion, Scotland's first batch of German and Austrian Jewish refugee children reached Central Station, 'to be temporarily adopted in Jewish homes in Glasgow'. In reprisal against persecution of co-religionists in Nazi Germany, Glasgow's Jewish traders boycotted German goods – including furs, silk stockings and women's fashions. Scottish members of the Spanish Republic's anti-fascist International Brigade, along with thousands of sympathisers, filled the City Hall, Candleriggs, to pay tribute to 500 volunteers killed in Spain.

After the Empire Exhibition closed, a rumour circulated that demolition squads were taking on extra workers. Five hundred desperate jobless men – 'from almost every corner of the city' – rushed to Bellahouston Park. Sentences of 60 days were imposed on members of the Derry Boys, the Nunny Boys and the Baltic Fleet. In Bridgeton, the Norman Conks and the Shanley Boys fought a pitched battle, using bayonets and hatchets. After the Methylated Spirits Act came into force, numbers of meths drinkers arrested in Glasgow fell from 610 in 1937 to 78 in 1938. A middle-aged woman fell into a blanket held by people in the street when she attempted to jump out of a first-floor flat in Bellgrove Street, Camlachie. She told a court: 'All I wanted was a fish supper.' Overhead tramway wires saved the life of another woman who overbalanced and fell from a window of a tenement in Duke Street. The Rev A.N. Davidson, minister of Glasgow Cathedral, wanted Kelvingrove Park closed after dark – 'in the interests of propriety'.

1939   Hitler: 18s

Glasgow Corporation distributed 'anti-gas protective helmets for babies'. The Corporation employed more than 1500 men to erect Anderson steel air-raid shelters in back gardens in city housing schemes. Lord Provost Patrick Dollan suggested: 'A good old-fashioned tenement is as safe an air-raid shelter as can be found.' When Glasgow's air-raid sirens were tested, 'citizens had difficulty hearing the warbling note, especially when traffic roared past'.

A Glasgow detective posed as a blind man in order to nick a street bookie in Maryhill. IRA terrorists were suspected of concealing 51 sticks of gelignite in a public toilet at Anderston Quay. The vestibule of the City Chambers was converted into a National Service recruiting office. One of the first volunteers was Sandy McKinnon (84). Glasgow's 300ft 'Tower of Empire' in Bellahouston Park was sold to a scrap merchant. An unemployed man got six months for holding up a shop girl at gunpoint and stealing sixpence. Two young Scottish Nationalists were charged with tearing down a recruiting banner.

Swears and Wells, furriers, Sauchiehall Street, offered 'antelope swaggers' at three guineas. Glasgow Corporation voted to emulate Vienna and build 'model working class tenements'. Speaking at the Highlanders' Institute, Mrs Billington Greig suggested wives should be paid for housework. After war broke out on 3 September, black-out regulations left Glasgow 'dark as a wayside hamlet, with not a single light shining'. At a Glasgow auction, cinema magnate A E Pickard paid 18s for three portraits of Hitler.

Glasgow ARP authorities called for 'protective caves in hilly districts which offer natural slopes as suitable sites.' Magistrates promised to consider allowing publicans to employ barmaids to replace barmen called up for military service. It was reported that 'women are taking fewer risks than men in city streets during black-out hours'. Ayr Town Council heard that many evacuees from Glasgow possessed only the clothes they arrived in. Many Ayr women had to burn the clothes of evacuated children and re-outfit them at their own expense. It was alleged that evacuated children were 'treated like cattle' by Aberdeenshire farmers.

At Nash's ARP Equipment Store, Union Street, citizens could order 'Anything from a Twopenny Bandage to a Fire Engine'. A Glasgow businessman was fined for storing 10 gallons of petrol in his tenement flat.

1940   Cheeky Forty

Glasgow students Charities Day featured 'Hitler's Storm Troopers and Nordic Maidens'. Women shoplifters caused an 'epidemic' of thefts of silk stockings. John McDaid and Andrew Kane were jailed for robbing a poultry farm in Great Western Road, under cover of the black-out. Officials claimed window-smashing in housing schemes had increased as a consequence of the black-out. Chief Constable Percy Sillitoe predicted that the black-out, combined with closed schools, would lead to a juvenile crime wave.

Glasgow's first hillside air-raid shelter was cut into a steep incline in Springburn Road. It could accommodate 300 people in six large brick-lined bays. Glasgow Corporation voted to build 1500 houses at Hillington, to accommodate incoming essential war workers from England. Glaswegians suffering from overcrowding protested at the plan. Thomas McDougall threatened a Garngad shopkeeper with the attentions of the Cheeky Forty gang. McDougall got 12 months for extortion. A number of ventriloquists' dolls were among donations to Glasgow's War Relief Fund.

Daly & Sons, Sauchiehall Street, offered 'Anti-Concussion Helmets' – supposedly designed by a 'nerve specialist' to protect the ears and skulls of Glaswegians from 'blasts and concussion from bombs'. Mr and Mrs Ditscher, St Vincent Crescent, advertised their 'Deutsche Sprachschule'. The couple emphasised they were citizens of Switzerland. The Northern Fur Stores, Buchanan Street, urged: 'Buy a Fur Coat and Keep Warm and Calm in Your Air-Raid Shelter.'

As more men were conscripted, Glasgow magistrates lifted their 30-year-old ban on employment of barmaids in city pubs. J C Sinclair & Co, Wellington Street, offered 'ARP Self-Adhesive Masking Tape – Prevents Poison Gas Penetration, Seals Instantly Doors, Windows and All Apertures'.

As Nazi armies smashed through Allied defences in the Low Countries, the Cosmo Cinema featured *La Grande Illusion* – an anti-war classic. More than 20 German and Austrian women were rounded up in Glasgow following a Home Office instruction that 'women aliens' were to be interned. Glasgow women responded warmly to a civic appeal for voluntary relief workers to assist with reception of Belgian and Dutch refugees. In the aftermath of Dunkirk, French-speaking Glaswegians were asked to visit wounded French soldiers in city hospitals. Hundreds of city children were evacuated to camps in rural Lanarkshire and to Aberfoyle. For almost the first time in history, the city had a 'stay at home' Glasgow Fair. Glasgow City Police recruited 15 young women. The force announced: 'More women will be recruited if the innovation is a success.'

1941   Spam and Treet

After a noisy party in an air-raid shelter in Gretna Street, Parkhead, a number of teenage boys and girls appeared in court. The magistrate told them: 'You must not turn the shelters into music halls.' During a bitter feud between neighbours in McDuff Street, Parkhead, one family barricaded the shelter to keep the other out. As part of a

'V for Victory' campaign, Glasgow buses and trams had the letter 'V' pasted on drivers' windows. Motorists also sported the letter 'V' in the windows of their cars.

Glaswegians queued to buy American tinned foods which included Spam and Treet. The Glasgow and West of Scotland Fruit Alliance tried to popularise 'Carrot Marmalade'. Glasgow Corporation welfare department reported that growing employment in war industries had substantially reduced poverty in the city. Two men died after falling into Queen's Dock during the black-out. An eight-year-old city boy, evacuated to Lochgair, Argyll, travelled 80 miles to see his mother – making an 18-hour journey on his fairy cycle.

At a meeting in Renfield Church, the Rev David McDougall denounced anti-Semitism. 'It is an amazing belief that Jews drink Christian blood and bake their Passover bread in the blood of a Christian boy.' Three members of the Sally Boys – from Salamanca Street, Parkhead – were fined £10 for attacking an East End men's club. Two of Glasgow's emergency fire stations were staffed by women fire-fighters – the first such installations in Scotland. Glasgow publicans fixed the price of a bottle of whisky at 17/6d – 'a new record'. The price of a pub hauf rose to 11d. Many pubs closed for half a day per week to conserve liquor supplies.

Fifty tons of broken glass were removed from Kelvingrove Art Gallery and Museum, after a bomb landed nearby. Pettigrew and Stephen advertised 'Safety Net – Excellent Protection Against Flying Glass' The store also touted 'Glass Substitute – Windproof and Weatherproof'. Three Eastenders – Nurse Cecilia McGinty, Dr J S McLaren Ord, and Dr Daniel Millar – were awarded the MBE for operating on a man trapped in the wreckage of a blitzed tenement in Allan Street, Dalmarnock.

A Glasgow man received 15 months' imprisonment for looting during salvage operations in the wake of the Clydebank Blitz. Twenty-seven employees at Copelawhill tram works were charged with failing to perform fire-watching duty. In what was dubbed 'Glasgow's saccharin ramp', traders charged tuppence for a packet of five sugar-substitute saccharin tablets.

1942   British Restaurants

Civil Defence authorities warned Glaswegians: 'Gas may come at any time. It will come as a complete surprise.' Glasgow Corporation turned down a suggestion from the Ministry of Works to demolish the Bridgeton Umbrella for scrap. As part of the 'Dig for Victory' campaign, thousands of citizens took municipal allotments for the duration of the war. Caviar, sent by the Soviet Embassy in London, was auctioned at Glasgow Fruit Market in aid of the Soviet Red Cross – and fetched £1 10s an ounce. A Glasgow Rabbit Club was set up to promote production of rabbit meat and pelts.

Smallpox – supposedly 'brought in a ship from Bombay' – resulted in Glasgow undertaking what was described as the 'largest mass vaccination campaign ever undertaken in the world'. Within a month, more than 500,000 citizens were vaccinated. The Ministry of Information was urged to combat 'Nazi lies about Glasgow'. Nazi Germany was supposed to be broadcasting 'news' that the city had thousands of smallpox cases. The dental health of Glasgow children was said to be 'deplorable'. Youngsters attending the city's dental hospital were described as 'in many cases, dentally beyond redemption'.

Glasgow women rushed to buy 'walking clogs' – with uppers of bright-coloured leather and light wooden soles. Responding to rationing of clothes, Glasgow Corporation education committee allowed girls to wear slacks at school. To save paper, city stores ceased wrapping purchases – resulting in an increase in shoplifting. It was claimed that peak-hour rushes to board Glasgow trams were so desperate that businesswomen had suffered 'torn clothes, bruises, and even broken limbs'. Citizens were urged to be hospitable to coloured seamen. 'These men are in the Merchant Navy, daily risking the hazards of the sea, facing death to bring us food.' The American Red Cross turned the Grand Hotel, Charing Cross, into a residential club for US service personnel.

Moral welfare campaigners claimed Central Station was 'infested by dozens of young girls'. A shebeen in Warwick Street, Gorbals, was reputed to be a favourite haunt of Polish servicemen. Two soldiers grabbed £47 from a Sauchiehall Street tearoom – and vanished into the black-out. An army deserter was jailed for stealing 62 bicycles 'left outside libraries and similar institutions'. In the city's British Restaurants – price and quality controlled, publicly owned eating places – a 1s lunch consisted of broth, stew and potatoes, and steam pudding. Glaswegians were said to be eating 'the products of their own parks'.

1943   Banana: £8

The director of Glasgow's American Red Cross Club claimed that US service personnel were obtaining raw liquor in city shebeens. Police arrested a Glasgow bridegroom as he arrived for his wedding at a Maryhill church. He was charged with stealing watches and other articles. It was alleged he'd stolen the items to pay for the wedding. Five boys took part in 'bombing escapades' – after stealing hand grenades from a Home Guard munitions dump. Three boys were charged with stealing 12 motor cars, two taxis, a van, and a naval lorry from the city centre. Glasgow's education department appointed two officers to interrogate school truants whose misdemeanours included 'forwardness in approaching servicemen in the streets'.

Glasgow councillor David Gibson offered to evidence 200 cases in Shettleston in which more than 10 people were living in one single-end. Police arrested 59 men at a pitch and toss school in Ardenlea Street, Bridgeton. Three men were charged with 'a ramp against the public'. They'd sold split pins 'bent to resemble genuine Kirbygrips'.

Notre Dame Child Guidance Clinic reported: 'Children are finding the departure of their fathers on war service a much more shattering experience than bombs falling outside their front doors.' Mrs Annie McLaughlin, a 41-year-old tram conductor, left to train as a welder. The city's Chief Constable claimed: 'Undesirable characters often mix with customers at coffee stalls in blacked-out streets.' Mrs Kidd, Springfield Square, Bishopbriggs, sold a banana for £8 – which she donated to a comforts fund for soldiers. Five repatriated Glasgow POWs celebrated their liberation by drinking a bottle of 'King's Ale' – brewed at Burton on Trent on the occasion of a visit by King Edward VII. It 'tasted like sherry'.

Glasgow Corporation had 96,000 housing applicants – including 800 families containing a person with TB. Thousands of citizens queued to see the 'Sword of Stalingrad' at Kelvingrove Art Gallery and Museum. Pettigrew and Stephen offered children's fur coats for £12 7/3d. The average weekly wage for a woman worker was £2 18/6d. A prisoner escaped from Barlinnie wearing clothes belonging to the governor. School children addressed some of the 1,100,000 rations cards issued to Glaswegians.

Lord Provost J M Biggar criticised women who 'instead of having children keep idle dogs which cause annoyance to gardeners and allotment holders'. Glasgow Corporation promised its post-war housing drive would meet 'the dreams of young couples'.

1944　　Khaki Panties

House-breaking in Glasgow increased. The authorities claimed this was a consequence of 'black-out conditions and scarcity of clothing'. Forty-six members of the Antediluvian Order of Buffaloes were fined £3 each for consuming unlicensed liquor in their Bridgeton lodge. Non-resident ward maids and kitchen maids in Glasgow hospitals earned £2 10s per week. Bridgeton Women's Club gave lectures on venereal diseases.

Adventurous Glaswegians varied monotonous wartime diets with off-the-ration food such as crow pie and pigeon pie. Rooks sold at 10d each. Pigeons fetched 3s a time. Addressing the Scottish Socialist Teachers' Society in Glasgow, nutrition expert Sir John Boyd Orr said: 'Britain's magnificent food policy is responsible for the fast growth in height and weight of Glasgow children. Today in wartime the poorest third of the population are actually better fed than before the war.' Crowds danced at Parkhead Cross and Bridgeton Cross when Glasgow introduced the 'dim-out' – a tenfold improvement on the black-out.

A 'Glasgow Home of the Future' went on show at Penilee, where Glasgow Corporation opened a demonstration block of prefabricated foam-slag concrete houses. Dr James Dunlop, Civil Defence medical officer for Glasgow alleged: 'Among Glasgow women of child-bearing age who suffer from tuberculosis, 70% are beyond human aid when their condition is notified.' Glasgow Corporation received housing applications from more than 24,000 homeless families. Supporting plans for temporary all-steel houses, Councillor Jean Mann stated: 'There are instances of Glasgow householders having to burn the gas all night to keep rats off their beds.' Parents were urged to make 'full use' of the city's children's clothing and footwear exchange in Kilmarnock Road. Garments were disinfected before reissue. Parachute Regiment CQMS Walter Semple (30), Possilpark, became one of the first Allied soldiers to land in Normandy on D-Day. A company director was jailed for three months for resetting 300 pairs of khaki panties. Householders were advised: 'Thanks to dried eggs you can have at least six nourishing egg dishes every week. If you are four grown-ups in a family your allowance of dried egg is two packets a week.' Government released for civilian use a limited quantity of penicillin. Glasgow Royal Infirmary reported the new drug's use as 'wonderfully successful'. James Thom was jailed for two years for stealing 400 gallons of whisky from Eglinton Street goods station. City transport supremo E R L Fitzpayne suggested 'underground trams' as a solution to post-war inner-city traffic congestion.

1945   Frau Jean

Police claimed reluctance by gang-attack victims to give evidence handicapped efforts to halt the East End's 'razor slashing epidemic'. Three city youths who broke into Glasgow warehouses and offices were living rough in an air-raid shelter in Dennistoun. Two married women house-breakers were jailed for stealing clothing, money and jewellery from houses in Bridgeton. An 11-year-old boy and several of his 8-year-old pals stole a car and went on a 'joy ride'.

The Post Office launched a campaign against evasion of radio licences – and 15,000 new licences were purchased in the Glasgow area. Miss Euphemia Mackay – at 5ft 1in, Glasgow's smallest policewoman – nabbed a 20-year-old man who tried to steal an army lorry in Queen Street. Glasgow businessman Hamilton McIntyre attacked plans for a national health service. 'Planning is something that came from Germany,' he declared. It was claimed that 'lack of footwear' accounted for truancy from Glasgow schools. Two city youths were caught wearing fur coats they'd taken in a smash and grab raid on a city furrier's premises. A condemned tenement in Portland Street, Gorbals, was described as 'a menace to life and limb'. Thirty-four families, comprising 56 adults and 73 children were still living there. They had nowhere else to go.

On VE night, Glasgow was reported a 'blitz of bonfires'. Newspapers claimed: 'Every central street in the city was like an approach to Hampden Park on a football international day.' Predicting the city's future, Lord Provost James Welsh envisaged 'Glasgow Green thronged with pleasure-seeking citizens watching great regattas on the Clyde'. Margaret McGregor (17) returned to Possilpark after five years as an evacuee in Ontario. Staff Sergeant Smythe, Dennistoun, was among the first British soldiers to enter Belsen concentration camp.

Newspapers reported that in the ruins of Adolf Hitler's Chancellery in Berlin, Allied investigators found a black folder containing fan letters sent to the Führer during 1936, by a Glasgow housewife who signed herself 'Your little Frau, Jean'. It was claimed the Gestapo had made inquiries of the City of Glasgow Police, who identified 'Frau Jean' as a 'well-connected middle-class woman'. VJ Night crowds were described as 'bigger than on VE Night'.

A baby girl was found abandoned in a close in Inverkip Street. At a meeting in the American Red Cross Club, 250 Glasgow 'GI brides' were presented with a book entitled *A Bride's Guide to the USA*. Glasgow Corporation offered householders the opportunity to buy their Anderson shelters at £1 a throw.

Part III
1946–1978

1946   Sten Guns and Dance Halls

Police raided a gambling club in West Nile Street. More than 200 punters were carted off in Black Marias. Charles Frederick Kepple was fined £50 for operating an illicit still in a store at 463 Argyle Street. On the annual Orange Walk, women outnumbered men by four to one.

At White City greyhound track, angry punters hurled bottles and stones at the judges' box and tried to storm the totaliser. At Maryhill Police Court, the area's Bantaskin Street was described as 'a den of gambling'. Fines ranging from ten bob to £2 were imposed on nine men who admitted playing pitch and toss in the street.

Argyle Street and Sauchiehall Street were claimed to be 'happy hunting grounds' for handbag snatchers. Glasgow department stores trained salesgirls in 'speech and etiquette'. The manageress of Lewis's Polytechnic, Argyle Street, where near-ly 1000 girls were employed said: 'We give voice culture to our staff because we think it is important.' Glasgow had 93 dance halls, almost three times as many as London in proportion to population. Biggest was the Dennistoun Palais, which held 1700 people. Next was Green's Playhouse, with a capacity of nearly 1300.

The number of squatter families in Glasgow was 'rising rapidly'. Squatters took over military camps at Balmore Road, Lambhill and Crookston. They also occu-pied a former 'model' in Govan Road, and Kelvindale House, a 24-room mansion in the West End. Twelve squatters were each fined £3 or 10 days' imprisonment for taking over an empty tenement in Lethamhill Road. They were charged under the Trespass (Scotland) Act 1865. At a meeting of Glasgow Homeless League, its president, A G Armstrong asked: Is there any person here today who would object to living in a Nissen hut?'

A Glasgow woman and her railway employee husband refused to claim newly introduced Family Allowance. 'We were brought up in the Scottish spirit of inde-pendence. We don't want charity.' Glasgow Jewish Sabbath Observance Society played host to 40 boys, survivors of Nazi concentration camps. The first big batch of GI brides left Central Station en route for the USA. One of the brides was Boston-bound Mrs George Baldasarre, formerly Miss Wilma Cloughley of Bishopbriggs.

Glasgow police took charge of a range of weapons, including rifles, revolvers, automatic pistols, sten guns, grenades – and an anti-tank gun. A few months before his death, Gorbals-born former world flyweight champion Benny Lynch was inviting customers of a Paisley Road pub to punch him in the face for the price of a drink.

1947   A Good Pair of Legs

Mrs Annie Healey, 22, gave birth to a daughter in a police box in Lorne Square. Alexander McArthur, co-author of *No Mean City* was found unconscious some distance from his room and kitchen flat in Waddell Street, Gorbals. He died in the Royal Infirmary. McArthur lived all his life in Gorbals and became a baker after leaving school at 14. Glasgow had 11,982 notified cases of TB – one in 12 of them from chronically overcrowded Gorbals.

City girls objected to long skirts introduced by fashion guru Christian Dior. 'What's the use of having a good pair of legs and coupon-nylons to match if you are going to hide them?' complained Miss Grace McDonald, Abington Street, Maryhill. James Cooke, 17, was so enthusiastic about army life that he changed places with his absentee soldier brother and even did 28 days' detention for him. A court heard James was anxious to be a soldier while his brother had no such inclinations. He was fined £1.

Fascists were blamed for anti-Jewish activity in Govanhill. The word 'Jew' was painted in huge letters across windows of local shops. Glasgow's Hindus and Moslems celebrated in Hillhead Burgh Halls to mark the creation of the self-governing nations of India and Pakistan. A Bell Model 47 helicopter – the first to reach Scotland – arrived in Glasgow aboard the Anchor liner *Eucadia*.

A self-styled 'Atlantic air-pilot' called at a city pub and conned customers out of £5 by promising to supply smuggled nylons within 48 hours. The Ministry of Labour asked Glasgow hospital matrons to consider employing girls from the continent – officially termed 'displaced persons' – as domestic workers. Glasgow built its first 'domestic skyscraper' at Crathie Drive, Partick. It contained 88 flats for single women. Mourners helped dig graves when city grave-diggers went on strike for an increase of £1 a week.

At Glasgow Sheriff Court, Charles McDonald asked for time to pay a £15 fine. There was a man in court who'd travelled from England to tell him he'd won

£26,000 on a football pool. Scots comedian Will Fyffe, who made famous the song *I Belong to Glasgow* died after falling from a hotel window. He was buried in the Western Necropolis, Maryhill.

Lewis's Polytechnic, Argyle Street, advertised stemmed wine glasses – 'the first since 1939'. Dr Blodwen Lloyd told Glasgow Association of University Women: 'We might look forward to the day when a woman is Prime Minister.

1948   Chip Shop Bandits

Gorbals and Hutchesontown Housing Association alleged that 'shady rent collectors' were 'backed up by razor gangs'. Tenants paying extortionate rents for rat-infested slums risked being beaten up if they took cases to rent tribunals. The four Neill children – Katrine (6), George (7), Jim (9), and Betty (13) emigrated to Southern Rhodesia, without their parents. Their father said: 'They are better away from tenement life, and will be given a better opportunity abroad.'

Sir Hugh Roberton, conductor of Glasgow Phoenix Choir, said: 'Military conscription is the deadly enemy of culture.' A diamond worth £250, a US 200-dollar bill, two brooches valued at £600 – and a live monkey – were among items held by City of Glasgow Police lost property department.

The first Australia-bound post-war emigrant ship, the *Empire Brent*, left Glasgow's King George V Dock, with more than 900 passengers. Councillor D W Gibson told a conference of the Independent Labour Party that eight women and 25 children were daily turned out of Foresthall Institution to walk the streets until evening. Potato rationing ended at midnight on April 30. Detectives stopped a man leaving Plantation Quay – because his figure was 'out of proportion'. He had 20lbs of tea in a sack tied behind him.

Wartime 'utility' furniture piled up 'unwanted' in Glasgow shops. Three men were accused of stealing 72 hens from a farm in Nitshill Road. Throughout the city, thieves stole safes or blew them in situ. Police raided a house in Cavendish Street, Kingston, and found 76 detonators, nine sticks of gelignite and 16ft of fuse. Glasgow police sought 'fish restaurant bandits' who'd robbed chip shop proprietors at gunpoint.

Annie Keenan, 60, found drunk and incapable, made her 31st appearance at Maryhill Police Court. The fiscal said: 'It used to be beer and whisky for Annie.

Now she is reduced to methylated spirits.' At Govan Police Court, a known thief and former member of the Beehive gang asked for his army record to be taken into account. Fiscal: 'You were a deserter?' Accused: 'Yes, sir.'

More than 300 children from 52 schools left Glasgow on five special trains for potato-harvesting camps in Perthshire, Kincardineshire, Ross-shire and Argyll.

A railway worker was held up at gunpoint by three young men who took his cigarette case, removed the fags, and handed it back. Little Tories were on display at a 'Unionist Baby Show' in Pollokshields.

1949   Sweeties and Squatters

Eight people died after drinking hooch at a New Year party in Queenslie Street, Blackhill. When clenny worker Joe McFadyen emerged from a close in Greenhead Street, Bridgeton, a colleague noticed the fins of a mortar bomb protruding from Joe's refuse basket. A month before the Greenhead Street incident, Joe had found a live hand grenade in a bin in Dalmarnock Road.

Commander T D Galbraith, Tory MP for Pollok, extolled spanking for boys and girls up to the age of 18. 'It hurts but it doesn't do any harm.' When sweets rationing was temporarily suspended, children rushed to buy the first non-rationed sweets since 1942. In five minutes at one sweetie shop, Nora Thompson (9) spent 5/6d. She explained: 'When I came out of church I called on Uncle Fred, Auntie Nell, Grannie and Grandad, my two married brothers and my sister, and they all gave me money for sweeties.'

Miss Ruth Clarkston, Matron of the Sick Children's Hospital, Yorkhill, complained that almost half of the hospital's 400 beds were vacant because of shortage of nurses. Pulmonary TB caused 1093 deaths in Glasgow.

An army ambulance rushed squatter Mrs Rita Russell from Hallhill military camp, Baillieston, to Duke Street Hospital, where she gave birth to a baby girl. Twelve days later, mother and daughter returned to the camp – and the baby was refused admission because she wasn't on the official list of squatters. Dr T J Honeyman, director of Glasgow's art galleries, condemned cocktail parties as 'the lowest form of social activity I have ever known'. Isabel Saxeby (6) Possilpark, became the 100,000th UK emigrant to arrive in Australia.

Citizens flocked to Kelvin Hall to view the 'Glasgow Today and Tomorrow' exhibition. Centrepiece was a scale model of the city in 1999. Organisers predicted: 'Helicopters will take off and land from the flat roofs of grand new railway termini.' Clerks, labourers and artists were among applicants interviewed in the Central Hotel for the post of Scotland's first 'male mannequin'. A three-month-old boy was found on the steps of the chapel house at Dalbeth Convent, London Road. A note pinned to the baby's clothes read: 'I am sorry I have to leave the baby at door. I have no place to take him to, as I have tried every place for him.' After workers ripped off the roof and removed all doors and windows from a condemned tenement in Shamrock Street, Gorbals, 14 families of squatters remained in the building. They had nowhere else to go. The squatters included a blind girl aged four.

1950   Blood and Red Biddy

In 1950, 'Glasgow Christian Commandos' targeted city factory workers. 'The few Communists who tried to disrupt meetings were shouted down by their fellow workers.' Split £1 notes were offered in city post offices. One assistant said: 'I unfolded it and, noticing it felt a bit thin, turned it over and saw the back had been peeled off.'

Glasgow's police surgeon urged visitors not to be scared of the city. 'The average picture of Glasgow – blood-stained razors, streets flowing with blood and red biddy, and a town in which no man or woman could move about with safety – is far from being correct.' City grocers claimed blackmail by customers trying to obtain extra tea rations. One trader complained: 'Tea might be a drug which has got them in its grip, judging by the tricks they try to wheedle a little extra. One woman burst out crying when I refused her tea in advance. Another tried to bribe me with cigarettes.'

Passing a resolution noting with regret that municipal trams and buses were carrying ads for football pools, Glasgow presbytery of the Church of Scotland described pools as a 'great social evil'. A small boy, playing on waste ground near his Dennistoun home, found a shoe box wrapped in brown paper and tied with string. The box contained a newly-born baby boy. The baby, still alive and crying lustily, was rushed to the Royal Maternity Hospital, Rottenrow.

Police attempted to take into custody a donkey which had disrupted traffic in busy Castle Street. Officers made 'noises calculated to coax stubborn donkeys into Black Marias', but the animal refused to budge. A total of 2950 Glasgow school pupils left the city to help with the potato harvest. Glasgow Corporation's school attendance committee refused to allow harvest supervisors to inflict corporal punishment on school-age tattie howkers. Thieves hid themselves in the George Cinema, Crown Street, Gorbals, waited until the cinema was closed and blew the safe, escaping with nearly £100.

Glasgow men were reported as 'the most hat conscious in Britain', after a 'hat census' was taken at a busy city street crossing. Out of 1000 men counted, 67.1% wore hats. Calling for 'discipline with no nonsense about it', Bailie Edwin Donaldson, chairman of Glasgow's education committee, opined: 'Original sin is born with the child. It has to be trained out.'

1951   Promoting Immorality

Charlie Miller (81) employed in a Keppochill iron foundry, celebrated his 70th year as a moulder. He'd started work in a foundry at the age of 11. The 'squeezie', a room kept in darkness at Glasgow University Union during 'Daft Friday' dances, came under suspicion of promoting immorality. 'There being a room in total darkness within the Union during a dance can only serve to bring the utmost disrepute on every Union member, to say nothing of the legal aspect of the matter.'

Bailie John Johnston described Progressive Party plans to build and sell 622 council houses at Merrylee as 'class legislation with a vengeance'. At a stormy protest meeting in St Andrew's Halls, cheers greeted Leslie Foster, a young building trades shop steward, when he stated that the houses would be built 'over our dead bodies'. Expert safe-cracker Johnny Ramensky (45) was jailed for five years for blowing a safe in Cardonald post office. During WW2, he'd served with the commandos, blowing safes behind enemy lines. His fall from grace after the war, said his defending counsel, was 'caused by debt and the fact that his prison record made it hard for him to get work'.

There were 32,477 single-ends in Glasgow – and 106,794 room and kitchen homes. Families who became homeless after the collapse of a tenement gable end in Lambhill Street, Kinning Park, were offered temporary accommodation in Glasgow Corporation's Foresthall Institution – a former poorhouse. Pulmonary TB caused 674 deaths in Glasgow.

An official of Glasgow Remand Home, 264 St Vincent Street, claimed: 'Some children so enjoy the food, cleanliness, craft work and film shows that they want to go back to the home after being released.' Glasgow police raided two shops and seized 900 'obscene books'. Some of the books were about American gangsters. Ordered to quit condemned property in Cavendish Street, Gorbals, squatters attempted to take possession of huts at Cowglen Military Hospital.

Glasgow Corporation's transport committee debated the question: 'Should men who have been tram drivers and who are now conductors be asked to collect fares on trams driven by women?' The committee agreed that because of a shortage of male recruits, 200 conductresses with more than five years' experience should be allowed to train as drivers.

1952   Telly Tickets

Cranhill building workers returned New Year greetings cards from Glasgow's housing convenor, as a protest against the Progressive Party-controlled Corporation's decision to sell Merrylee council houses. Shop steward Edward Donaldson said: 'More cards would have been returned, but most were immediately torn up and flung away in disgust as soon as they were read.' In March 1952, when television came to Scotland, there were fewer than 1000 licensed TV sets in Glasgow. Jamaica Street store Arnott-Simpson invited customers to view TV – 'admittance by ticket only'. Sauchiehall Street trader Biggars offered sets from 49 guineas. Average weekly wage was £7 7/3d – with many Glaswegians earning less.

William McFadyen was jailed for five years for firing pistol shots that wounded two people in Union Street. He claimed he opened fire to deter 'a notorious Bridgeton gang called the Billy Boys', who were pursuing him. Police took fingerprints from the male population of Garnethill, after the murder of four-year-old Betty Alexander, whose body was found in Buccleuch Lane. Her killer has never been identified.

Glasgow art students protested against the proposed £8,200 purchase of Salvador Dali's 'Christ' painting for the city's art gallery. They claimed: 'The money would be better spent establishing a gallery where young artists might exhibit periodically.' A gang of youths attacked and robbed Indian pedlar Mohammed Hayat in London Road, escaping with his case containing nylon stockings and silk head squares. Thieves stole a lorry loaded with 80 cases of rationed tea from the Clyde Shipping Company, Calton Place.

In Bath Street, ex-servicemen queued to join the Australian army, which wanted 1000 recruits. The recruiting officer said: 'it looks like we might get them all in Glasgow.' Citizens whose homes overlooked the Forth and Clyde canal watched Royal Navy midget submarine XE9 en route from Garelochead to Rosyth.

City transport supremo E R L Fitzpayne promised tram services 'for many years to come'. Townhead women with scrubbing boards and placards marched to the City Chambers to demand reinstatement of a condemned steamie in Collins Street. Glasgow had 6511 'able-bodied unemployed'. A prisoner escaped from Maryhill police office by knocking a hole in the ceiling of his cell. James Robertson, Glasgow's assistant Chief Constable, suggested: 'If there were more old school ties there would be less delinquency.'

For the second time in her life, six-month-old Georgina Hamilton was bitten by a rat in her tenement home in Richmond Street, near Rottenrow Maternity Hospital. A 'blitzkrieg' of the City Chambers by jet bombers was the highlight of a massive civil defence demonstration in George Square.

1953   Skyscraper Flats

To celebrate the Coronation (June 2), public buildings were floodlit, fireworks displays were mounted in city parks, school children were given a three-day holiday, and old folk in Corporation homes received 5s each. Shortly before the event, a young man climbed 20 feet up the facade of Copeland and Lye's department store in busy Sauchiehall Street and removed the numerals from an 'E II R' sign, clambered back to street level, and vanished into the crowd. Messrs Copeland and Lye stated that since they erected the royal cipher they had received several threatening telephone calls and letters demanding its removal.

An experimental machine in the Cancer Research Laboratory at the Royal Beatson Memorial Hospital in Hill Street was reported to 'smoke' ten cigarettes at a time and get through 10,000 fags per year. The dark tarry residue was fed to laboratory mice. Asked if cigarettes were a health risk, Dr P.R. Peacock, in charge of the experiment, said: 'I don't know if smoking is dangerous, but it might be.'

Hundreds of spectators gathered in the Temple district of the city to watch a pitched battle between two rival gangs. Police reinforcements were rushed to the scene from Maryhill. As the neds fled, they left a trail of weapons in their wake. 'The whole population of the district seemed to have turned out to watch the fight,' said a police spokesman, 'and the streets were black with people.'

More than 40 passengers were injured when a No. 22 tram jumped the points in Commerce Street, Tradeston, crossed Kingston Street, and crashed into a railway bridge. Although injured, conductress Rose McGuinness (20) took a prominent part in the rescue work. The driver, Elizabeth McGibbon, was among those detained in the Victoria Infirmary.

Glasgow scenes of *Highland Fling*, a film about a Clyde puffer, began with American actor Paul Douglas entering the Central Hotel and continued with footage shot at the docks. The film, in which a fifteen year old Govan boy, Tommy Kearins, starred as a member of the puffer crew, was later released as *The Maggie*.

The first tenants moved into Moss Heights, 'skyscraper flats' at Craigston. The flats were let at £2 7s per week. Months after moving into their flat in Moss Heights Avenue, Alex Millikin and family had to move out again when water poured into their flat after heavy rainfall. Another family complained: 'We get water coming through the walls even when there is no rain'.

Glasgow Corporation voted by 23 votes to 16 to keep a sculpture of a dancing nude mother and child on the wall of Chirnsyde Primary School in the Milton housing scheme. The sculpture, a composition in reinforced concrete, had previously been described as 'pornographic'. Urging the Government to ban American comics, Glasgow schoolteacher Archibald Neil opined: 'There is an exaggerated emphasis on sex and violence in this type of paper. The law is flouted on every page. Superman is superior to the law, which is brought into contempt.'

1954   The South Side Vampire

Dr Zevedi Barbu, lecturer in social psychology at Glasgow University, claimed: 'When a Scotsman kicks a football he imagines he is kicking his father's head.' Thieves escaped with £187 after blowing a safe in the manager's office at the Picture Palace, Tollcross Road. They used carpets and the assistant manager's dress suit to muffle the explosion.

Glasgow Marriage Guidance Association offered lectures on 'the physical relationship in marriage'. Young couples attending were 'not a bit embarrassed'. Directors of the Blythswood Shipbuilding Company, Scotstoun, searched in vain for a bust of Helen of Troy – whose face 'launched a thousand ships' – for their boardroom. The firm settled for the bell from an oil tanker. Residents in Caledonia Road, Gorbals, called police to complain about a disturbance caused by hundreds of children pouring into the Southern Necropolis to track down and slay 'a vampire with iron teeth'. Bailie John Main claimed American horror comics were responsible for the 'vampire' scare. He wanted city magistrates to ban the comics.

Dr Stuart Laidlaw, Glasgow's medical officer of health, criticised 'sausage manufacturing in small, ill-ventilated back shops' in Govan. He claimed that in one instance sausages were made 'in a small cupboard beneath a staircase'. Miss Mary Margaret Macauley, Victoria Park Drive, was crowned 1954 Candy Queen. Her prizes included a cheque for £100, a £50 trousseau, a weekend in Paris, and a week's stay at a holiday camp. An off-duty Glasgow police officer chased two men he'd seen trying to break into a shop – and was batoned by another officer who arrive in a patrol car and took him for a villain.

1955   Squalor and Tellies

While renewing woodwork surrounding the 'jawbox' sink in his home at 14 Ronald Street, Robert Tipping (23) found a box containing 65 Scottish £1 notes, 48 half-sovereigns and four sovereigns. Latest date on the notes was 1912. Blackhill was described as 'Glasgow's worst housing scheme'. The city factor claimed pitch and toss schools, gang warfare, razor slashings, and consumption of cheap wine were rife in the scheme. A police officer commented: 'There's a saying, "money's as scarce as stairhead windows in Blackhill".'

At Moss Heights, Cardonald, a quarter of the 267 flats were untenanted and awaiting repairs. Councillor John Forrester said: 'Despite the inconvenience suffered through water penetration, most people are satisfied with their houses.' MacTaggart and Mickel offered three-apartment houses in Kelvinside, Giffnock and Newton Mearns, from £1710.

A Glasgow teacher told a conscientious objectors tribunal: 'I refuse to be conscripted because I feel I must be able to decide myself what wars are justified.' It was reported that the city's smoke pollution was at its worst at Glasgow Cross. Air at Belvidere Hospital, London Road, which treated cases of pulmonary tuberculosis, was 'only slightly less polluted'. US evangelist Billy Graham addressed mass rallies at Kelvin Hall, Ibrox Stadium and Hampden Park. After the campaign, Glasgow bookshops reported: 'Bible sales are breaking all records.'

US pop star Johnny 'Singing in the Rain' Ray appeared at the city's Empire Theatre. Teenagers 'screamed and yelled and all but tore their hair'. Two days before he was to be executed at Barlinnie, freelance writer John William Gordon was granted a reprieve. Gordon had been convicted of murdering Glasgow radio star George McNeill – who played 'Mr McZephyr' in radio soap opera The McFlannels – in the actor's tenement flat in Water Row, Govan Cross. Gordon's landlady in Scott Street, Garnethill, recalled her lodger's carefully typed short stories. 'They were on the theme of abnormal relationships between men. And they all had the same ending – murder.'

The Glasgow committee of the Royal Scottish Society for the Prevention of Cruelty to Children claimed: 'Squalor and television sets – even cocktail cabinets – have been found in the city in the same houses as neglected children.' Despite opposition from churches, Glasgow Corporation allowed Sunday bowling in city parks. In Glasgow's Kingston district, women claimed to be afraid to go out at night because they feared attack in 'poorly gas-lit side streets'. Glasgow's policy of 'no pubs in housing schemes' took a knock after a Lanarkshire licensing court approved a pub in Springboig – near Barlanark and Cranhill. The Corporation's finance committee rejected a plan to preserve as a restaurant and arts centre the former Cranston's tea rooms, Ingram Street – designed by Charles Rennie Mackintosh.

Civic leaders forecast a 'major housing crisis' unless agreement was reached on building a new town at Cumbernauld – 'to take the city's surplus population'. Fraser's, Buchanan Street, offered 'sheerest nylon stockings' at 11/6d a pair. For the 12th time, smash-and-grab thieves raided shirtmaker Joe Fletcher's St George's Road shop. 'I think it proves my shirts must be pretty good,' said Mr Fletcher. 'I refuse to put iron grilles on my window. It makes the place look like a zoo.'

E R L Fitzpayne, Glasgow's transport manager, claimed: 'The increasing number of motor cars on the roads are almost paralysing the centre of the city.'

During a High Court trial, a witness explained that 'Malky Fraser' was gangland slang for an old-fashioned cut-throat razor.

1956   Worse Than Hong Kong

Three thousand city children, many wearing imitation racoon-skin hats, mobbed Lewis's Polytechnic, Argyle Street, to catch a glimpse of US film star Fess Parker, famous as 'Davy Crockett – King of the Wild Frontier'. An elderly man went into a Govan Road café and asked for an empty bottle – which he then used to carry out a smash-and-grab raid on a nearby pawnshop.

A Glasgow doctor expressed disgust at 'squalor and misery' in the city's 'models'. 'The cubicles are so small I can hardly move, and the lighting is so dim I can hardly see the patient.' Govan's MP, John Rankin, claimed scores of the area's slum houses were 'far worse than in the Chinese quarter of Hong Kong'. In one close in Hoey Street, 70 people shared a toilet.

After watching *Rock Around the Clock* – starring Bill Haley and the Comets – at the Tivoli Cinema, Partick, hundreds of teddy boys and girls danced in Keith Street. Near the Embassy Cinema, Shawlands, 'young couples were whirling madly under the sway of the rhythm-provoking chanting of the crowd'. At the Gaumont, King's Park, 'A number of regular patrons were disgusted at the shouting and stamping during the screening.'

After a rat bit six-year-old Annette Wilson in Florence Street, Gorbals, her mother said: 'I've lived in this house for 14 years, and the place has been infested with rats all that time. My husband has caught more than 40 rats in the house.'

In Balornock, Barmulloch and Robroyston, agitated parents found their children playing with 300 sticks of gelignite they'd found in a derelict brickworks. Glasgow Corporation announced that in rebuilt Hutchesontown-Gorbals – the city's 'future dream town' – only 57 shops would be provided in place of the existing 440. There would be only nine pubs compared with the existing 47. Pettigrew and Stephens, Sauchiehall Street, offered 'three-piece television suites' at £22 10s.

Eleven days after his wife, daughter and sister-in-law were found shot dead in the family bungalow in High Burnside, William Watt, managing director of Denholm Bakeries, was arrested and charged with the triple murder. After 67 days in Barlinnie, he was released. The real murderer – Peter Manuel – was still at large. Glasgow clergymen were attacked by teetotal Lord Provost Andrew Hood. 'We can no longer look to a great many of them for a lead in the important question of temperance or total abstinence.'

1957   Rock'n'Roll Socks

Twenty-one-year-old Bridgeton-born 'Queen of Skiffle' Nancy Whiskey played her first big gig in her home town, at the Glasgow Empire. Ironmoulder John Anderson, Culloden Street, Dennistoun, saw two 'flying saucers' from the top deck of a tram near Govan docks. 'They were perfectly round and shone like two silver threepenny bits.' Public health officials tested 142 beer glasses in 50 city centre pubs. Only 19 were 'reasonably clean'.

Glasgow launched a mass X-ray campaign, using 36 mobile units to 'get at the hard core of TB infection'. In five weeks, 712,860 people were X-rayed. Bailie John Mains said: 'The figures achieved in Glasgow will go down in medical history.' Digging was suspended at a filling station in Gorbals when workers unearthed several incomplete skeletons. Suspicion of foul play was allayed when detectives discovered the site had formerly been occupied by St Ninian's Hospital for Lepers – founded in 1345.

Police fought to control fans after Bill Haley and the Comets appeared at the Odeon Cinema, Renfield Street. Groupies chanted 'We want Billy' and waved banners reading 'Bill Haley, he's the most.' Councillor S J Scott Anderson complained: 'The modern three Rs are rock'n'roll, record playing and radio.' A young man wielding a sheath knife robbed a Gorbals drapery shop – and made off with two pairs of 'rock'n'roll socks'.

James Quail (38) living with his wife and eight children in a 14ft by 8ft single-end in Rosemount Street, Garngad, refused to leave – despite warnings that the tenement was in danger of collapse. 'I am not leaving here until I get a house. I refuse to go to Foresthall, the Corporation home. Since 1949 I have had my name on the Corporation housing list. Why can't something be done to get my family out of this squalor?' Eleven families were left homeless when part of a wall of a condemned tenement collapsed in Gemmell Street, Bridgeton. Some went to Foresthall – others to friends and relations.

'Heavenly Rapture' and 'Atomic Energy' were among titles used in a handbill from a city grocer advertising bottles of cheap red wine. Male students of the Royal College of Science and Technology staged a 'pantie raid' on a women students' hostel at Jordanhill Training College. Mrs Elizabeth McPherson, Camden Street, Gorbals complained: 'Rats have eaten up half the floorboards. At night my husband and I watch them running about the room. Some of them are as big as cats.'

1958   Three Tries for Gentleman Johnny

Glasgow safe-blower Johnny Ramensky – behind bars for 21 of his 53 years – escaped three times from Peterhead prison. On his third attempt, he was at liberty for nine days. 'Gentleman Johnny' had escaped from Peterhead twice before – in 1934 and 1952.

Police took charge of a black and white cow which had wandered into a tenement back court in Birnam Road, Tollcross. Instruments valued at £1,000 and 9,000 musical scores were lost when fire destroyed Glasgow's famous Barrowland Ballroom. The last passing out parade of the Highland Light Infantry took place at Maryhill Barracks. The regiment was amalgamated with the Royal Scots Fusiliers to form the Royal Highland Fusiliers.

Six homeless families – one of them with a seven-month-old baby – squatted in the vestibule of the city's health and welfare department in Montrose Street, after walking out of Foresthall – a former poorhouse used as emergency accommodation by Glasgow Corporation. Expectant mother Mrs Mavis Taylor said: 'Nothing will induce me to go back to that home. I couldn't stand it another night.' A meeting of the British Women's Temperance Association heard claims that schoolboys in Glasgow's West End went to pubs during their dinner hour. 'They put on coats over their blazers so they can be served.'

Knightswood community centre was branded as an 'eyesore'. Started in 1937, it remained unfinished more than 20 years later. Bridgeton-born comedian Tommy Morgan died at his home at Kelvin Court, Anniesland. Five out of every 1000 Glaswegians had bacillary dysentery – partly because of widespread use of communal WCs in old tenements.

Glasgow Corporation approved architect Sir Basil Spence's 'revolutionary' scheme for multis in Gorbals. The city's housing convenor said: 'There is no design like this in this country or anywhere else.' Teenage girls – most of them in care because of bad home circumstances – escaped from Lochburn Home, Calder Road, Maryhill. They alleged ill-treatment at the home. The first three Glaswegians were fined £2 each under the new Litter Act.

Mrs Isabella McHale, one of the first tenants of the new Hutchesontown-Gorbals redevelopment scheme said: 'After 20 years of sharing an outside lavatory, I'm in seventh heaven at the very thought of a bathroom to ourselves.' Peter Manuel was convicted of murdering seven people. After Manuel's execution, plaster casts of his face went on sale in Glasgow – at 10s a time.

1959   Drams For A Dug

Hong Kong-born Mr Wong Chong opened 'The Chinese Restaurant' – described as 'completely and thoroughly authentic' in Sauchiehall Street. Tom Easton (19) climbed to the top of a 60ft ash tree – the only tree in Argyle Street – to rescue a stranded ginger cat. Tenants in Drumchapel housing scheme were promised 'decorative pools and ornamental fountains' when their long-awaited shopping centre was eventually built.

City whisky magnate A B Grant offered £100 and a crate of Scotch for the safe return of Skipper, his wife's lost poodle. The dog made its own way home. Malaya-born Mrs Marira Gilfillan, who'd allegedly never left her Maryhill Road flat since 1938, said 'I see all I want of the world from my window. I'm happy this way.' Marira had been brought to Glasgow as a bride in the 1920s.

Customs officers found more than 62lbs of Indian hemp on board the cargo ship *Prome* during searches in Glasgow and Greenock. A police spokesman denied Glasgow was becoming an HQ for drugs gangs. 'There are no dope gangs centred in Glasgow. But there are contact men used to pass the drug on to gangs in the London and Liverpool areas.' A newly born baby girl, found lying on the floor of a communal WC in a tenement in Sandyfaulds Street, Gorbals, was taken to the Royal Maternity Hospital, Rottenrow. More than 2000 local authority delegates at an 'overspill problem' conference were told: 'Half the houses in Glasgow have only one or two rooms and over 400,000 people are living in them.'

Detectives searching for Samuel 'Dandy' Mackay, who'd escaped from the hospital wing of Barlinnie prison, believed the wanted man had grown a beard and was 'posing as an artist'. Labour Lord Provost Myer Galpern was criticised for sending his son to exclusive fee-paying Gordonstoun School. Mr Galpern said: 'Gordonstoun treats all boys the same – they don't care who the parents are.' Gorbals MP Alice Cullen claimed that, in the Royal Maternity Hospital, women were left in beds in a corridor to await ambulances to take them home within hours of giving birth. A hospital spokesman said: 'Women in labour are never turned away, even if they have to be put up in corridors.'

1960   Colour Bar City

Fourteen Glasgow fire-fighters and five members of the city's Salvage Corps died in an explosion which destroyed the west side of Arbuckle, Smith and Company's whisky bond in Cheapside Street, Anderston. It was Glasgow's worst peace-time fire. The bond contained £6,300,000 worth of whisky.

Silent crowds lined city pavements and traffic halted as fire-fighters marched to Glasgow Necropolis – where the Cheapside victims were buried in a common grave. City firemaster Martin Chadwick demanded removal of whisky bonds from densely populated areas. 'During the war, we asked for bonded warehouses to be moved from the city centre because of the possibility of fire during air raids. This was done. But since the war they have moved back into the city.'

Urging Glasgow landladies to accept coloured students as lodgers, the Rev Martin Magee said: 'One agency which helps students find accommodation told me that out of 1000 landladies on their list only 50 were willing to take coloured students.' At a rock'n'roll tribute to singer Eddie Cochrane, in the Empire Theatre, Billy Fury and other UK performers were pelted with bottles and metal ashtrays. Twelve angry families refused emergency accommodation in Foresthall after fleeing a collapsing tenement in Tennant Street, Townhead. Said one tenant: 'Nothing seems to be done until the place falls about your ears.'

After a city murder trial, during which Queen's Park recreation ground was described as 'a haunt of perverts', police estimated there were at least 10 times more assaults and robberies in the park than were reported. 'Because of the nature of the incidents many victims don't report them,' said a police officer. The Rev Adam Clark, minister of the nine-member Church of God, Maryhill, took The Word to Polmadie brickworks, where vagrants slept in vaulted kilns – 'still warm after the bricks are removed'.

City magistrates recommended citizens should have an extra 15 minutes' 'drinking up' after closing time at 9.30pm. Mrs Jean Roberts, Labour councillor and former teacher, became Glasgow's – and Scotland's – first female Lord Provost. Glasgow Corporation passed plans for the Ladywell housing scheme – on the site of Duke Street Prison – and agreed to take over Maryhill Barracks and build multi-storey blocks on the 54-acre site. The new Barrowland Ballroom opened at the Barras, in time for Christmas. Top of the bill were 'Billy MacGregor and his Gaybirds'.

1961   Barlinnie Badges

A Govan gents' outfitter offered 'Barlinnie blazer badges' – with a motto reading 'Ad Sum Ard Labour'. Glasgow Valuation Court heard that houses in Garnethill were 'being used for immoral purposes'. Glasgow had more licensed betting shops than any other city in the UK – 407 compared with London's 293. Mrs Iolanda Simone or Gherardi (59) was fined £110 for shebeening at her Argyle

Street flat. Since 1958, she'd paid about £700 in fines.

Fire ended the 99-year history of the Metropole Theatre, Stockwell Street – founded in 1862 as the Scotia Music Hall. Advocating removal of Glasgow's Tolbooth Steeple from the roadway at Glasgow Cross, Councillor Peter McCann opined: 'To have it stuck in the middle of one of the busiest streets in one of the busiest cities in the country seems silly.' Glasgow Young Socialists marched to Greenock Prison, demanding release of anti-Polaris demonstrator Pat Arrowsmith. Commenting on Glasgow's lack of H-bomb shelters, the city's civil defence officer said: 'The Glasgow tenement, with its thick stone walls, takes you a long way towards having a ready-made shelter.'

Glasgow safe-blower 'Gentleman Johnny' Ramensky was transferred from Peterhead to Edinburgh's Saughton Prison. At Billy Graham's Ibrox rally, about 800 people made 'decisions for Christ'. Organisers issued 100,000 tickets – only 37,000 people attended. Speaking to the National Vigilance Association in Glasgow, the city's ex-Chief Constable Sir Percy Sillitoe blamed books such as *Lolita* and *Lady Chatterley's Lover* for 'looseness of morals, particularly in young girls'.

John Shannon (15) became the first delivery boy to supply city office workers with coffee and sandwiches. His Wellington Street employer hoped to have more than 20 uniformed delivery boys. An 18-year-old youth landed in Glasgow Royal Infirmary with eight broken toes after wearing Italian-style 'winkle-picker' shoes. Thieves 'rustled' a British Railways mechanical horse, laden with 80,000 cigarettes.

Cracksmen used table-covers to muffle the blast when they blew a safe in Walter Hubbard's tearooms, Dumbarton Road. Ten-months-old Elizabeth Walsh was bitten by a rat in her home in Thistle Street, Gorbals. Her father said it was not unusual for rats to come out and sit watching him eat his lunch. When a police officer visited the house, a rat scampered across the floor in front of him. The constable threw his baton at the rodent – but missed.

1962   Some Guy!

Mrs Iolanda Simone or Gherhardi – Glasgow's 'Shebeen Queen' – was evicted from her Argyle Street flat. She'd been fined more than £1000 for shebeening. Neighbours had complained that taxis arrived at Iolanda's close 'at all hours of the night'. Veteran city anarchist Guy Aldred – 'the knickerbocker politician' – polled 134 votes as an Independent Socialist in a by-election in Glasgow

Woodside constituency. Aldred first entered the electoral arena in 1922, when he stood for Shettleston. He held the UK record for lost deposits.

Citizens paid 2/6d each to travel on 20 trams, which left Ruby Street depot, Dalmarnock, in a ceremonial last tram procession to Coplawhill depot. An estimated 250,000 people lined the streets or watched from tenement windows. Thousands risked injuries by putting pennies on the tracks in order to obtain misshapen souvenirs of the occasion. Jail-breaker and safe-blower Johnny Ramensky came out of prison on five days' parole under a 'training for freedom' scheme. He went home to his wife's flat in Eglinton Street, Gorbals.

The Rev Geraint Jones described conditions for boys at Mossbank approved school, Millerston, as 'something out of Charles Dickens'. Twenty anti-nuclear demonstrators took part in a 48-hour protest fast outside Glasgow Cathedral. Fifty families were evacuated from tenements in Kent Road and Granville Street when fire destroyed world-famous St Andrews Hall. City branches of Radio Rentals Ltd offered portable transistor radios for 13 guineas cash. City Cash Tailors, Saltmarket, advertised Italian-style suits for £3 5s.

Tenants complained about vandalism in Royston's new 18-storey multis. They claimed that common rooms – intended as 'centres of social life' – had become 'junk stores and lavatories'. After 12 years on the housing list, Bill and Catherine McCafferty moved with their children from a rotting tenement in Pine Street, Hutchesontown, to a multi in Commercial Court.

Dressed in brown shirt, black tie and Sam Browne belt, Glasgow bank clerk Arthur Smith claimed to be the 'Scottish Führer'. Ex-soldier Smith said: 'I formed the group 15 years ago but we have kept underground all these years. Now we have an increasing number of followers and it will soon be time to come out into the open.' Bungalow and villa owners in 'Old' Drumchapel demanded rates reductions. They claimed that since the construction of Drumchapel housing scheme, their lives have been blighted by traffic, smoke, gangs of children, and drunks. Glasgow Corporation approved plans for multis in Ibrox, Knightswood, Dalmarnock and Balornock.

1963   Orgies and Budgies

Glasgow Corporation ordered removal of the city's remaining WW2 air-raid shelters. There were still 100 public surface shelters, 7000 Anderson shelters, and 2000 communal backcourt shelters in the city. The final curtain fell at the city's Empire Theatre – infamous as 'the graveyard of English comedians'. Police raided Carntyne Casino in the East End. 'Elegant fur-coated women and tuxedo-clad men' were carted off in Black Marias.

The death was reported of Alex Goodwin (70) a former cinema musician who'd played the violin in Glasgow streets for 34 years – since the 'talkies' had put paid to cinema orchestras. When he began busking, Alex wore a mask to conceal his identity. The Pets' Pampery, a beauty salon for dogs, opened in Bath Street. Said proprietor Nicol Watt: 'Glasgow's dog owners are becoming more and more beauty conscious where their pets are concerned. As many as 400 dogs will be treated each week and I'll have a staff of 11 girls to help me.' Special feature of the salon was a 'Budgie Hotel' – providing lodgings for pet budgerigars.

Chuck and Gideon, real names Iain Campbell and Leonard Kelly, Glasgow's answer to the Everly Brothers, made their first disc – *The Tender Touch*.

Townhead councillor James F Reilly claimed: 'The public don't realise that in some houses in Glasgow some disgusting orgies are taking place as a result of the drugs and other things used by coloured seamen.' Drumchapel celebrated its 10th anniversary with a 'Birthday Week', the official opening of a new shopping centre with a 'futuristic fountain', and the slogan 'Let Drumchapel lead each noble deed.' The scheme housed 40,000 people – comparable with the city of Perth.

Safe-cracker 'Gentleman Johnny' Ramensky (57) who'd spent more than 30 years of his life behind bars, was released from Saughton prison, after serving eight years of a 10-year sentence. To speed up slum clearance and give employment to shipyard workers, Glasgow Corporation ordered 34 'homes on wheels' from the Blythswood Shipyard, Scotstoun. The first 'home on wheels' was erected in Greenhead Street, Bridgeton.

After complaints from people who'd been on Glasgow Corporation's housing list for many years, the Corporation appointed a 'hush-hush' committee to investigate allegations that well-heeled local government officials had been allocated 'luxury flats' at Balcarres Avenue, Kelvindale. Beneficiaries included the £1145-a-year- curator of the City Chambers and a traffic commissioner earning £3400 per annum. The latter paid a subsidised rent of 13s a week for his flat.

1964   Beatnik Styles

Easterhouse tenants seeking transfers out of the scheme cited 'the rising incidence of lawlessness and vandalism' as reasons for wanting to move. Veteran safe-breaker Johhny Ramensky was jailed for two years for trying to blow a safe in a Woolworth's store. His lawyer said: 'He does not seek wealth or position, merely the right to work and live as a human being.' Two-thirds of the families who'd been rehoused in the new Gorbals petitioned Glasgow Corporation asking for a ban on pubs in the area. Said councillor Frank McElhone: 'They want to avoid the old conditions of public houses next to their houses.'

Beatles fans overturned cars and smashed shop windows when the Fab Four appeared at the Odeon Cinema, Renfield Street. Boys with Beatle haircuts were banned from public baths in the city if they refused to wear bathing caps. The manager at Townhead baths said: 'They simply won't get in if they don't bring their caps.' 'Purple hearts' were among stolen 'pep pills' circulating in the city.

Six months after his death, veteran Glasgow anarchist Guy Aldred – who had died with 10 pence in his pocket – was cremated at Maryhill Crematorium. Believing all his life that human existence consisted of service to others, he'd left his body to the anatomy department of Glasgow University. Glasgow Corporation reversed its 1890 resolution banning pubs in city housing schemes. The ban on singing in pubs was also lifted. The Corporation had feared trouble in pubs from singing of sectarian songs.

A 63-year-old Partick shopkeeper was fined £20 for erasing the Egg Marketing Board's 'lion' stamps from eggs – in order to pass them off as 'fresh farm' eggs. Pettigrew and Stephen, Sauchiehall Street, offered ladies' stretch nylon pants in 'beatnik styles' for 9/11d. Glasgow Corporation agreed to buy 950 parking meters for a pilot scheme in the city's Blythswood Square area. Highways convenor Jerry O'Sullivan said: 'The experience throughout the country is that meters do something to alleviate parking problems.'

Nineteen-storey multis in Rutherglen Road, Gorbals, were 16 months behind schedule. Designed by Sir Basil Spence, the concrete-built flats were to feature 'hanging gardens'. Said one local: 'They're an eyesore. They don't look like houses at all. And what about that colour scheme – blue and orange. That's going to cause trouble for a start.' West End Misfits offered 'tail suits for Masonic functions – from £7'.

1965   See Ya Later Alligator

A Knightswood family quit their council house and moved in with relatives – where they shared a room with five other people. The family had complained about neighbours holding noisy parties. In reprisal, the exterior of their house – including doors and windows – was covered with orange paint. At least 30 people, including a number of children, were found living in a slum flat at 381 London Road, Calton.

Film comedian Norman Wisdom announced his ultimate dramatic ambition – to play tragic Glasgow-born boxing hero Benny Lynch. Wisdom said he was particularly interested in re-enacting post-WW2 incidents in which the once-great flyweight had been reduced to giving skipping demonstrations for the price of a drink. Witnesses in a number of Glasgow murder trials refused to give evidence – stating they were afraid to do so.

During 1965, no fewer than 11 spiritualist churches regularly advertised services in various parts of the city. Ads for Eldorado proclaimed 'Demand Growing Daily!' A woman parked her pram outside Goldberg's department store, Candleriggs, and entered the shop with her baby. When she emerged, she found a three-month-old abandoned baby boy asleep in the pram.

Celtic FC boss Jock Stein warned that increasingly rowdy behaviour by fans could lead to the club's permanent closure. Dr Maurice Miller, Labour MP for Kelvingrove, wanted Glasgow's Asian bus drivers and conductors sent to 'repopulate the Highlands'. Mrs Janet Barbour, Glasgow's only female 'coalman', took up selling briquettes from a cart pulled by her white horse Nancy. Councillors met to arrange the transfer from gang-ridden Drumchapel to sought-after Knightswood of a council tenant whose name was not mentioned during the brief housing committee meeting. Drumchapel residents – many thousands of whom were on transfer lists in hopes of escaping from the scheme – exploded with fury when it was later revealed that the lucky tenant was Labour councillor Constance Methven.

In June 1965, a Springburn woman received a letter from Glasgow Corporation. She had applied for a council flat – in 1926. The letter asked if she wanted to renew her application. City taxi driver Tom Ferguson, Castlemilk, got a call to Glasgow docks – where a foreign seaman wanted a tour of the city. Mr Ferguson's customer sat in the back of the cab nursing a two-foot long live alligator. Back at the docks, the sailor admitted he couldn't pay the £2 fare. Mr Ferguson took the alligator as 'security' and sold it to a city pet shop – for a fiver.

1966   Councillors' Holidays

A Dalmarnock man wrote to a newspaper agony aunt. 'My girlfriend chews gum even when I'm kissing her. I don't like the taste, so it puts me off.' It was estimated that up to 100 shilling-in-the-slot meters were robbed in Glasgow every weekend. Four luxury mansions owned by Glasgow Corporation water department at Loch Katrine were kept as exclusive holiday homes for city councillors. Councillors paid 6/6d a week for use of up to 10 bedrooms, two-car garages, free electricity and a speedboat. Asked whether poor city children might not benefit from such holiday facilities, Labour councillor Constance Methven said: 'We daren't run the risk of polluting the water.'

In Easterhouse, dozens of desperate people queued every morning at the scheme's housing office – to seek transfers out of the area. Garscube Colliery, Summerston – Glasgow's last coal mine – closed with the loss of 350 jobs. A bomb exploded in the car of gangster Arthur Thompson, killing his mother-in-law. Thompson survived. He had only driven 10 yards from his 'fortress' house in Provanmill Road. John Glaister, former professor of forensic medicine at Glasgow University, declared his opposition to hanging – which he deemed a 'barbarous practice'. Glaister wanted murderers poisoned in prison – 'at a time unknown to themselves'.

Police reported a spate of thefts of umbrellas in the city. The brollies were sought after as fashion accessories by mods. George the coal horse took off at a fast canter – complete with loaded cart – in Greendyke Street, Calton. In nearby Charlotte Street, the cart smashed a car belonging to a city man James MacGregor. Mr MacGregor said: 'I phoned my wife to tell her a horse had run into the car. Good job I'm a teetotaller – or she wouldn't have believed me.'

Neds stole a single-decker bus in Govanhill and abandoned it after crashing into a lorry – 100 miles away in Tarbert, Argyll. Bearsden residents objected angrily to plans for a chip shop in the affluent suburb. One woman said: 'If we have one of these shops here we would get all the undesirables in.' Jimmy Pye (78) died at Foresthall Corporation home. He had entered Foresthall in 1910 – when it was a poorhouse. His estate consisted of a picture of a woman on a hill, a piece of medal ribbon and a tattered empty envelope.

1967 Ties with Lally

Tenants in Possilpark described their scheme as 'Glasgow's second Blackhill'. A quantity of heroin and morphine was taken during a break-in at a pharmaceutical store at Victoria Infirmary. Scout troops in Glasgow mounted a drive to attract boys from Indian and Pakistani backgrounds. A spokesman said: 'We don't expect immediate results.'

Glasgow City Labour Party threatened to expel councillors who sought an end to fee-paying in some council schools. Glasgow Corporation education department was short of 1300 teachers, with 2500 children receiving part-time education – many of them in Easterhouse. Veteran safe-blower Johnny Ramensky was jailed for four years after robbing a bank safe.

A Glasgow shop manager named Patrick Lally refused to withdraw from sale 'blood red' ties bearing a heraldic shield enclosing crossed swords and the gang motto 'Ya Bass'. Mr Lally, described as a 'Labour Councillor', claimed the ties were 'only frivolous'. The convenor of the city's police committee said: 'Anyone who sells goods of this kind is doing a disservice to the city.' Police officers also condemned the ties.

Top art dealers in London and Paris anxiously sought the whereabouts of Glasgow-born artist Scotty Wilson (76). At the age of 50, Scotty – described as a 'wizened eccentric' – had discovered his ability to draw. He had become an internationally regarded surrealist artist. Scotty would sell his drawings to passers-by at £1 a time – outside posh art galleries asking huge prices for his work.

At the Odeon Cinema, Renfield Street, James Bond – played by David Niven in *Casino Royale* – raised a shotgun and aimed at an on-screen grouse. At that precise moment, a Glesca pigeon flew across the screen. The delighted audience yelled: 'Ye missed!' Cinema manager John Murray said he'd been trying to catch the pigeon for a week. 'I nearly caught him the other night. There he was – sitting in one of the best circle seats.'

Glaswegians were reported to be leaving the Church of Scotland at a rate of 4000 a year. Two years after rescinding an 1890 resolution forbidding pubs on municipal property, Glasgow councillors agreed to a limited number of pubs in Easterhouse and Drumchapel.

1968   That Bastard Boyle

The manager of the Locarno Ballroom, Sauchiehall Street, challenged young Glasgow women to take part in the 'Goose-Pimple Walk'. The walk involved bikini-clad girls taking a 200-yard stroll along Sauchiehall Street – in near-zero temperatures. First prize was a fortnight in Majorca. Winner was Connie Wilson (20), Ledmore Drive, Drumchapel.

'Baby-faced killer' Jimmy Boyle – convicted of murder in 1967 – was done for assaulting the assistant governor of Barlinnie Prison. Armed police foiled a gangland plot to free Boyle on his way to court. Gang lawyer James Maxwell Latta was jailed for conspiracy to give false evidence for the defence at Boyle's murder trial. One of Latta's co-accused said: 'This is what you get for trying to help that bastard Boyle.' It was revealed that Glasgow had accounted for 41% of violent crime in Scotland since 1963.

Pakistan-born university graduate Sardar Khan (30) became Glasgow's first ethnic minority traffic warden. Labour councillors refused to implement a government order to abolish fee-paying at selective Glasgow Corporation Schools. Nearly 4000 children were receiving part-time education – none of them at fee-paying schools. As Glasgow Roman Catholic archbishop James Scanlon walked to the lectern to read a lesson at an inter-church service in Glasgow Cathedral, Pastor Jack Glass – 'Ian Paisley's official representative in Glasgow' – sprinted along the nave, shouting 'This is Popery!'

After a January hurricane damaged hundreds of Glasgow tenements – causing a number of fatalities – soldiers were posted to prevent looting of furniture and shilling-in-the-slot gas meters. Scottish Nationalists Malcolm McCormick (24), Clarkston, and Neil Gow (18), Busby, climbed scaffolding on a building in St Vincent Street – and removed a banner reading 'I'm Backing Britain.'

An ambulance crew raced to respond to a 999 call from Glendale Street, Bridgeton – and ran into a close to help the 'casualty'. Minutes later, their ambulance was driven off by neds. It was found in Baillieston – on its roof. In the aftermath of Ne'erday 1968, 350 Corporation Transport employees failed to turn up for work. Another 560 phoned in sick. The Corporation had to take 280 buses off the road. A survey alleged every resident of Drumchapel and Easterhouse wanted to leave the schemes. Tennent Caledonian Breweries were refused permission for 'mannequin parades' at pubs in Possilpark and Springburn. A councillor said: 'Can you imagine what would happen if the girls paraded in mini costumes?'

1969 Colin Stein x 3

Blackhill's 15 streets were described as 'the grimmest, toughest, most lawless estate in all Scotland'. Research revealed that Blackhill had 1971 registered criminals – out of a total of 1152 families. Truancy in the scheme was attributed to the huge number of adults who, rather than escort children to school, permanently stayed at home to guard their gas meters and furniture.

Renfrewshire County Council demanded that Glasgow send only 'good quality' tenants to the new town of Erskine. It was reported that private developers in the new town feared a collapse of property values if 'low quality' Glaswegians moved in.

Ex-RAF pilot James Callan, Loskin Drive, Milton, was bequeathed the Iron Cross belonging to a German pilot he'd dragged from a crashed Stuka in North Africa in 1942. He hadn't heard a word from the rescued man until receiving a phone call telling him about the medal.

Labour councillors attacked SNP councillor John Brady who'd remained seated during the Loyal Toast at a Glasgow Corporation lunch. Brady also wanted the Corporation to write to the Queen seeking £4m to build new houses in the city. 'I would like her to visit Glasgow,' said Brady. 'I could show her places in Bridgeton she wouldn't allow her horses and corgis to spend the night in.'

'Naked women' spotted on the roof of a building in Robertson Street turned out to be tailor's dummies placed there by tongue-in-cheek demolition workers. As a charity stunt, 400 students drank dry the Mally Arms, Eglinton Street. The students consumed 112 gallons of heavy, 132 gallons of lager, 45 gallons of stout, and 22 gallons of export. New-born Colin Stein Traynor, Copland Road, became the third Glasgow baby named after Rangers star Colin Stein.

Barras barber Joe Urquhart was given an absolute discharge after being charged with cutting hair on Sundays. A by-law of 1912 allowed only Jewish barbers to ply their trade on the Christian Sabbath. Vandals attacked the Calder Street, Polmadie, church of Pastor Jack Glass. Surveying the damage, Glass blamed 'religious fanatics'.

Giving evidence in a case at Glasgow Sheriff Court, a prostitute told a sheriff that she didn't work weekends. She admitted there was more money to be made at weekends. 'But that's when I stay in to watch the telly,' said the witness. It was claimed that little boys living in Glasgow's multis – and who couldn't get outside to play – would grow up over-attached to their mothers.

1970   Baroness McAuslane

Dozens of Glasgow children converged on a Maryhill scrapyard, after the drawer of a rusty till had been found to contain £1000 in cash. An eyewitness said: 'When the word "money" was mentioned, the children appeared from nowhere.' Nearly 20% of boys applying for apprenticeships at Upper Clyde Shipbuilders could neither read nor write.

Homelessness charity Shelter was refused permission for a flag day in Glasgow – after the group proposed to collect cash in strategically placed chanties. Sheriff officers forced their way into a Nitshill council flat, to poind the effects of council tenant Mrs Helen McAuslane, who owed £46 to the Corporation housing department. For years, Mrs McAuslane had styled herself 'Baroness McAuslane'. Her daughter was known as 'Lady Helen'. The baroness claimed she'd inherited her title from her own mother. Attacking the Corporation's action, the baroness said: 'People have no respect for the aristocracy.'

Cons in Barlinnie were alleged to be blootered on hooch made from tattie peelings and orange peel. A press informant added: 'And anything else they can get their hands on.' Glasgow Chamber of Commerce claimed businesses refused to invest in the city because there was too much rain. Investors were also afraid of 'having their throats cut in the streets.'

Youngsters in Maryhill and Bridgeton were accused of torturing cats and dogs by putting them on spits and roasting them on bonfires. The Scottish Society for the Prevention of Cruelty to Animals said 17 cases of 'animal barbecues' had been discovered. Most of the perpetrators were under the age of criminal responsibility. A mongrel pup died after neds threw it from a multi in Cranhill.

John Elliot (9) and his brother George (8) received certificates from the SSPCA for rescuing a kitten which had been covered in paint and bleach. 'Organised gambling' led bookies to refuse bets on dogs running at Glasgow's Carntyne dog track. It was revealed that one greyhound in five had been doped in order to rig races at the city's White City track.

Veteran Glasgow cracksman Johnny Ramensky was pushed into Stirling Sheriff Court in a wheelchair. He'd fractured his skull, thigh and wrist following a plunge from the roof of a building in the town. Eldorado was marketed under the slogan 'Be Good to Yourself'. A High Court judge described Glasgow as a 'city of weapons'. Razor slasher Robert Stewart was sent down for six years.

1971   Suitable for Church Elders

A survey of telephone box vandalism in Glasgow revealed only one phone box working in Easterhouse. A telephone engineer said: 'I wouldn't count on that one still working tomorrow.'

Tony Postlethwaite (60) of Pollok, got on his bike in an attempt to locate his missing Austin 1100. He had left it 'somewhere' after a night out with friends. He had even tried hypnotism in an attempt to find his vehicle. 'All I know is that it was somewhere in Pollokshields,' said Mr Postlethwaite.

Ads for Eldorado warned: 'Sip with Caution.' Glasgow's 3000 cabbies joined the Transport and General Workers Union, claiming city taxi owners were guilty of 'mass exploitation'. Bus conductresses Caroline Scappuccini and Maria Wilcox became the first female trainee drivers with Glasgow Corporation Transport.

Glasgow Chief Constable Sir James Robertson claimed there was no evidence of drugs problems among the city's student population. A sex shop – to be called 'Anne Boleyn' – was planned for Great Western Road. It was reported that the opening might be delayed as a consequence of blocked drains. Two hundred people, including four ministers, marched through the city in protest. The shop opened on 10 May. First customers were plain-clothes cops who removed several items to Maryhill police station.

Determined to maintain Sikh tradition for his nuptials, Mr Gurdave Singh Pall (21) rode a white horse from Pollokshields to claim his bride Raunindar Kaur at her Paisley Road West home. Rangers FC opened a new £500,000 social club – and discovered that barmaid Theresa McLaughlin (21) was a Celtic fan. 'If I get a Saturday off,' said Ms McLaughlin, 'I'll be at Parkhead.'

The Ruxton Bar, Elderslie Street, Anderston – earmarked for demolition – was sold to an international antiques dealer, who shipped it 4,000 miles to San Francisco, where its 80-year-old décor was recreated in a TV studio. The younger generation were being enticed into brewery-owned 'theme pubs' such as the Kimberly Queen,

Tollcross Road ('the realistic surroundings of an old man o' war') and the Tyrol, Argyle Street ('the atmosphere of a Tyrolean inn'). When 81-year-old former garage owner Alex Fairbairn died, his lock-up in Elmfoot Street, Polmadie, was found to contain a cache of corroded but valuable vintage cars and motor cycles, including a 1904 Talbot and a 1901 Scots-built Arrol-Johnson. West End Misfits offered gents' morning suits – 'suitable for Church Elders' – from £11.

Residents and shopkeepers in Blackhill housing scheme were promised the 'protection' of a police sub-station – complete with public telephone. Previous phones in the area had been wrecked by vandals.

1972   Barlinnie Bags

Sandy, the UK's first drug-sniffing Labrador, employed by City of Glasgow Police, found two packets of cannabis during his first operational outing. Neds broke into a day nursery in Civic Street, Maryhill, and stole two tortoises. Police said: 'Tortoise stealing is a fairly rare crime in the city.'

Veteran cracksman and prison escapee Johnny Ramensky was found not guilty of safe-blowing after forensic evidence was found to be faulty. It was the first acquittal in 'Gentleman' Johnny's 56-year career of crime.

Following a fire at a Parkhead cash and carry, 30 massive lorry loads of food were dumped at Garthamlock quarry, Gartlock Road. As newspapers hailed the advent of the 'affluent society', hundreds of residents began digging frantically through soggy ash and muck in an attempt to extract edible food. Police were unable to restrain the crowds.

Clutching bandages and blankets, nurses and doctors from Victoria Infirmary ran to assist a road accident victim outside the building. Chestnut, a carthorse belonging to scrap merchant Michael Reynolds, had been in collision with a lorry. Staff used sheets to stem blood from a gash in Chestnut's rump. He was conveyed to a vet's surgery in a horse box.

In the city centre, prostitutes from Newcastle fought with those from Glasgow. Prisoners at Barlinnie worked on a Scottish and Newcastle Brewers contract to make brown paper carry-out bags. Some of them fixed the string handles so that the bags fell to the ground when lifted. Others decorated the bags with obscene poems. The contract was cancelled.

Radio Free Scotland went off the air after police and post office investigators raided a flat in Leven Street, Pollokshields. Two hundred tenants of prefabs, built in 1949 in Sandyhills, campaigned angrily against council plans to demolish their homes.

Dr Herbert Kinnell, registrar in infectious diseases at Ruchill Hospital, was revealed as landlord of slum flats in Parkhead. Dr Kinnell – who began his career in property while a medical student at Aberdeen University – lived with his wife in a seven-apartment Bearsden bungalow. Tenants endured choked drains, toilets without seats and pools of filth in the backcourt. Glasgow Hospitals Northern Board of Management said: 'What Dr Kinnell does in his free time doesn't really involve the board.' A search of the city's valuation rolls showed Dr Kinnell as the owner of 41 flats in Glasgow. It was estimated that as a result of widespread closure of lodging houses, 500 people were sleeping rough in Glasgow during 1972.

1973   Nae Pick-pockets in Paradise

India-born Gulshan Singh, Paisley Road West, advertised himself as willing to teach other Glaswegians how to make curries in their own kitchens. 'The phone has been ringing non-stop since,' he said. Mr Singh added that a number of women had contacted his seeking him services as a male escort. 'It's a thought for the future,' said Mr Singh. It was claimed that students at Glasgow University had actually written much of the 'poetry' attributed to Victorian versifier William McGonagall.

Ibrox stadium had become a magnet for pick-pockets. Queues of drunks at refreshment stands were main targets. Police said: 'We have no problem with pick-pockets at Celtic Park.' An explosion seriously damaged the Apprentice Boys of Derry Club, Landressy Street, Bridgeton. The bomb consisted of nitroglycerine and ammonium chlorate, wrapped in waxed brown paper.

After inhaling shoe conditioner – said to be freely available at shops throughout the city – a 15-year-old boy was found lying in agony in a backcourt. He was described as 'howling like a dog'. Lord Provost William Gray enlisted '50 lovelies' to distribute 'Come to Glasgow' propaganda to London civil servants unhappy about transferring to Clydeside.

Unemployed labourer William McGillvray (35) of Maryhill, became 'Wilma McGillvray' following Scotland's first sex change operation. Factory chargehand Robert Adams announced that he was in love with 'Wilma'. They had met while working in the clenny.

Describing a flat at 180 Gallowgate, as 'almost uninhabitable', Glasgow Rent Assessment Committee slashed the rent drastically. The building was owned by the South of Scotland Electricity Board, which had applied for a rent increase. The building's common stair was lit by gas. It was announced that Blackhill would have a 'Gala Queen'.

Partick bride Lisanne Norman walked up the aisle at Downhill Parish Church to the accompaniment of a wedding march composed by her brother Richard (17).

Five cars were set alight in the yard at St Michael's RC Church, Parkhead. A number of other vehicles were daubed with the initials 'UFF'. Seven-year-old Norman Tait was so badly beaten up in a robbery in a close in Govanhill that he became unconscious and had to be rushed to hospital.

Police and fire-fighters conducted a massive search of ventilation tunnels and lift shafts at Queen Street station, after catering staff heard a young boy shout 'Mummy, daddy, help me.' Nothing was found.

1974   The Victoria Park Frogman

A fast-talking American showed up in Glasgow and announced high spending plans to build offshore oil rigs at Yorkhill Quay. He was lauded by press and councillors – and later turned out to be a penniless fantasy merchant. After yet another Old Firm punch-up at Hampden Park, councillors considered plans to acquire the facility through compulsory purchase – and use it for housing. One councillor said: 'We can put taxi drivers, dance hall operators, bookmakers and publicans out of business if they are in constant trouble. Why should football be any different?'

Three knife-wielding neds tried to hold up a bookie's shop in Gorbals. They fled when assistant Vera McDonald rang her mother Margaret Holland, who lived nearby. Mrs Holland rushed through the door intent on rescue – and the robbers legged it.

The City of Glasgow Police recruited its first ethnic minority policewoman, 19-year-old Sawamjit Matharu, who came to Glasgow from India in 1962. Police diver PC Tom Robbie searched the 2ft deep Victoria Park pond and found the lost wedding ring of Jane McLachlan, Dumbarton Road.

Glasgow University lecturer Dr Philip Hobsbaum – an Englishman – called Glasgow 'the worst town in the British Isles'. He said 'You are insulted if you walk into a pub and speak with an English accent. Theatre is virtually non-existent and films are a dreary diet of sex and horror.' Dr Hobsbaum added that he only stayed in Glasgow because university jobs were scarce elsewhere.

Foxes were reported in the ground of hospitals and shipyards in Govan. The nearby Shieldhall sewage works was home to a pair of mallard ducks. Other wildlife in Sunny Govan included kestrels, goldfinches, wagtails and fly catchers. Foxes were also reported in Oatlands – and one unfortunate fox plunged 200ft to its death from a multi-storey in Drumchapel.

Two dozen children, using picks and spades dug frantically for two hours to remove a ton of rubble from a floor in a derelict tenement in Gourley Street, Springburn. Stephen Sherrard (16) had heard howling from within the building. The children rescued a mongrel dog and her new-born pups trapped beneath the floor. Police said: 'It was great work by the youngsters. They saved Blackie and her pups from a terrible death.'

Tory councillors complained that official posters urging Glaswegians to use their votes in local elections had been printed in red – the colour used by the Labour Party. The council reprinted the offending posters – in orange.

1975 The Wee Effin

While appearing as a Womble at the Apollo Theatre, Renfield Street, London-based actor Patrick Scola chased a number of men down Clouston Street, Kelvindale, shouting 'I'll sort you out, you Scottish bastards.' His defence lawyer told a court: 'My client is a Womble. He unfortunately forgot that he came from Wimbledon when he drank Scottish beer at a New Year party.' Scola told reporters: 'I've lost my two front teeth and I feel sure I've let the other Wombles down.'

Ten families refused to leave condemned tenements in Gorbals – delaying construction by builder Crudens Ltd of multi-storey flats. Compensation to the builders cost the council £280,000. It was estimated that it would have been cheaper to buy each family an up-market house in the private sector.

Glasgow singer-songwriter Matt McGinn was charged with fly-posting to boost sales of his records. One disc was entitled 'The Wee Effin Bee'. A court dissolved into laughter when McGinn explained the title. 'Effin is a small town 942 miles outside Edinburgh. It's famous for its honey. So the place is full of Effin bees.'

Canadian-born Glasgow teacher Sheila Moberley was fired for wearing miniskirts at work. Describing her skirt as a 'pelmet', her colleagues claimed: 'It showed vast expanses of chubby thighs.' So many Glaswegians were travelling without tickets on the city's buses and trains that councillors claimed the entire public transport system was 'wallowing in debt'. Jobless teenagers – calling themselves the 'Right to Work Committee' – staged a sit in at Maryhill buroo. Unemployed engineer Doug Sharp said: 'We just got together recently to do what we could to bring attention to the problem of young people out of work.'

A female model, wearing only stockings, suspenders, briefs and bra, paraded in Argyle Street to advertise a new fashion floor at Lewis's department store. Police stepped up the hunt for Jackie – a male parrot missing from his cage in Waldemar Road, Knightswood. Jackie's owner, Kenneth Brown, toured the area with a female parrot called Jill. Mr Brown reckoned that 'sex-appeal' might reunite him with his missing pet.

Female students demonstrated outside Glasgow University Students Union against a strip show exclusively staged for male students. The show was billed as an 'anatomy lecture'. Jannies' houses at Queen's Park secondary school were attacked by vandals. Neds hurled bottles, bricks, chair legs, and dustbin lids. A half bottle of whisky smashed the bathroom window of jannie James Callender and his wife Ruby.

1976   Born on a Bus

Faced with a wave of vandalism in housing schemes, Glasgow District Council set up 'smash squads' to break windows of empty houses before the vandals did. After repeated break-ins at his pub, a Gallowgate licensee put up rolls of barbed wire at the rear of the premises. A few days later, the barbed wire was also stolen.

City councillors claimed an allowance of £10 each to watch a Government video on rabies. A leading record company promised to make Sidney Devine 'a household name throughout Britain'.

Staff at Sloans' Restaurant, Argyll Arcade, claimed the building was haunted by a ghost – believed to be the spirit of former owner Walter Myron. Walter was alleged to play the piano and brush against staff in corridors. Glasgow University

Senate refused to allow teenagers from housing schemes to attend classes. One lecturer claimed the idea was a 'Red plot'.

Convicted killer Jimmy Boyle complained bitterly that Strathclyde Police had placed two armed officers at his bedside while he was in hospital. The chairman of the Scottish Police Federation said: 'My heart bleeds.' Glasgow pick-pockets on holiday in Blackpool were arrested after stealing nine wallets containing a total of £419. The widow of city boxing champion Benny Lynch attacked plans by an England-based TV company to produce a play about the Gorbals-born pugilist. 'It makes Benny's mother appear to be a street walker. I'm going to write to the Queen.'

Elizabeth Proctor, Easterhouse gave birth to her son Conrad on a city centre bus. Mrs Proctor said: 'I'll never complain about waiting for a Corporation bus again.' A four-year-old boy started school in Priesthill. His mother feared some difficulties. His father had insisted that the lad was to be christened Henry Robert Geronimo Milligan.

It was revealed that Glasgow had 457,000 sub-standard houses, and that 44,000 people were on the council's waiting list. A report claimed Glasgow would become a city almost solely occupied by poor or elderly people – and would have 30,000 empty council houses by 1981.

Unemployed funeral director Scott Greene, Springboig, possessed 3500 books on Native Americans, along with an armoury of bows and arrows. He had learned to speak Souix and had become an adopted member of a Souix tribe. Mr Greene also claimed the US government had warned him off campaigning for the rights of Native Americans.

1977   Asbestos And The Birch

City councillors agreed to view a documentary film showing acts of vandalism and culminating in a staged birching scene. Conservative councillor Helen Hodgins wanted to bring back birching. 'If it was done in private the offender would be birched on the uncovered bottom. If the punishment was done in public, as I suggested for football hooligans, then the bottom would have to be covered or else it would be pornographic.'

There were calls for a full-scale investigation into allegations of drugs, drink and sex at Barlinnie prison special unit – after convicted killer Larry Winters, serving

36 years, died of a drugs overdose. Tenants in Red Road flats, highest in Europe, were warned not to interfere with ceiling tiles made of potentially dangerous asbestos. The city's housing director opined: 'The dust is only dangerous in large quantities and that will not happen if the tiles are not disturbed.'

Glasgow University law lecturer Philip Myers accused Glasgow District Council of using Blackhill housing scheme as 'a dumping ground for problem families, not only from the city but for families coming from outside if they have a prison record'. Cleeves Road, Priesthill, was described as a no go area. John Mann, chairman of the area's community association, said: 'Gang's are going about like packs of wolves there. Pensioners are scared to go out. Only a madman would walk up Cleeves Road at night.'

Paralysed and blind people, including Jessie Thomson, who lived with after-effects of polio, were among tenants stranded in a 24-storey multi in St Mungo's Place, Townhead, when maintenance engineers went on strike. Townhead residents also campaigned to save their steamie – one of 19 left in the city. The Co-op opened Scotland's first hypermarket at its listed HQ in Morrison Street, Tradeston.

Robert Storrie, manager of the Palaceum Bar, Edrom Street, Shettleston, made history – by becoming the first Glasgow publican to open his shop on Sundays. City pubs had been shut on Sundays for more than 120 years.

Glasgow District Labour Party restored the name of Patrick Lally to its list of council candidates. The former housing convenor had been deselected, following a letting scandal involving fellow Labour councillor Catherine Cantley. Mrs Cantley resigned when it was revealed she had 'used influence' to obtain a flat in exclusive Mansewood for her son and his girlfriend.

1978   Glue Sniffing

Glasgow travel agent George McClure offered trips to the World Cup finals in Argentina at £850 a head. Fans could borrow the cost via Provi checks. City entrepreneur John Higgins set up Glasgow's first custard pie and cream cake throwing service. At £30 a sling, Mr Higgins offered to 'squelch giant cream cakes into the faces of victims'. The service was ethically based, however. Mr Higgins declined to accept commissions for 'personal, political and business vendettas'. He explained: 'But other customers can have a choice of flavours. Strawberry, lemon, chocolate, you name it.'

West End resident Sue Reeve breastfed daughter Cathy in Hillhead public library. 'Two old men' complained to Glasgow District Council. 'The last thing I want is a feed-in at our libraries,' said civic amenities committee chairman Robert Logan. 'These women's libbers can be difficult.'

Glasgow woman Audrey Hepburn (23) became 'John Hepburn' after having her breasts and womb removed at Canniesburn Hospital. He/she was described as having 'the build of a typical docker'. A city pawnbroker was approached by a couple who wanted to pledge every piece of electrical equipment they possessed – including their stereo, TV, radio and food mixer. The would-be borrowers explained they were going on holiday and wanted to protect their goods from house-breakers.

The SSPCA was called in to trap foxes alleged to be digging up turf at Hampden Park. Glasgow safe-blower Paddy Meehan went into legit business – advising citizens on home security. The master lock-picker soon ran into a serious problem. He locked himself out of his car – and had to summon police to open the vehicle. Art student Katherine Grindlay went on a sketching assignment at Glasgow Sheriff Court. Sheriff Horsfall (50) invited her into his chambers for tea – and the happy pair soon announced their engagement.

City cinema managers summoned police to deal with a new threat – children who persistently sniffed glue during matinee showings. One manager said: 'They swear and shout and disrupt performances. When we stop them, they struggle with the strength of 10 men. They simply don't know what they're doing.'

Glasgow University psychology lecturer Ian Brown estimated that 60,000 Glaswegians had their lives blighted by chronic gambling. The city's TB rate was 32.9 per 100,000 people – compared with the Scottish average of 23 cases per 100,000 inhabitants.